Breaking Through

Loss

ONE POWERFUL STORY

ONE SCIENTIFIC METHOD

Lynn Hope Thomas

ISBN: 978-0-9870992-0-4 (sc)

Because of the dynamic nature of the Internet, any web addresses or links contained in this book may have changed since publication and may no longer be valid. The views expressed in this work are solely those of the author and do not necessarily reflect the views of the publisher, and the publisher hereby disclaims any responsibility for them.

The author of this book does not dispense medical advice or prescribe the use of any technique as a form of treatment for physical, emotional, or medical problems without the advice of a physician, either directly or indirectly. The intent of the author is only to offer information of a general nature to help you in your quest for emotional and spiritual wellbeing. In the event you use any of the information in this book for yourself, which is your constitutional right, the author and the publisher assume no responsibility for your actions.

date: 15/03/2019

First Published by Balboa Press in 13/11/2012

ISBN: 978-1-4525-0792-7 (sc)

ISBN: 978-1-4525-0793-4 (e)

Jeremiad

So they say

That change is constant;
Clearly we see
That life is otherwise.
With every seduction of time,
Souls embrace the wide arms of oblivion,
And pathetic it is to say
That the vault of my heart harbours hallucinations
Engendered by the memories of loved ones.
So they say
That who feels it knows it;
Winsome, the kisses of desolation was,
When death stealthily despoiled my heart.
On that saturnine day of acrimony,
In me, a shirty casualty was born;
Like the cleavage of dusk and dawn,
Serenity became a nightmare
As the umbilical cords of siblings were annihilated.
The love once known
Became a vain vapour
Saturating the atmosphere with agony
And without apt farewell fete.
What could it be
That life was trying to tell?
Like a miserable queen without diadem,
A cause to wonder was being fermented;
Lost I was on tenterhooks,
Not knowing how fate will thwack again.
Petrified, stupefied was I,
As the aghast melancholy became unbearable;
Electrifying souls dear to my heart are now wind

Traversing to a destination unknown
And never to return.
To the notorious namby-pamby foe of life, death
Luminous lasses of cheerfulness were lost;
Not even a gesture of cheerio was offered,
As my doppelganger sisters languish
Six feet beneath earth surface.
No one could understand the grief
I nurtured till this day;
In every twilight,
I yowl for the heavens to hear
The quavering in my soul
And the more I continued,
The more solace drifted away from my abode.
What could be said
That hasn't been said
To awaken the deceased from the grave?
I knew I was deadened,
But then reasoning spoke:
It takes courage to weep,
And another courage to smile;
My dauntless hope resurrected,
And to the glory of this day,
I lived for love and life.
In the abyss of the past
Lays my squabble with fate;
This lesson I learnt,
That the conundrums in every loss
Can only be answered
When hope is neither chastened nor stifled.
To home my twin sisters have returned,
But to the memories we shared,
I raise my hat high to the sky;
And in my heart,
They shall forever live, dear sisters.

Jacobs Adewale

TABLE OF CONTENTS

WHAT READERS ARE SAYING...

"When I started reading this book, I felt as if Lynn was talking directly to me in person. Her words are so authentic and certain, reaching directly my heart because every single word comes from the bottom of her heart. That was my first experience of feeling that way, although I have read many books. I also realised that people around Lynn in this book are "present" and "here" while I was reading. That is because she lives a world of transformation with love and gratitude rather than the one of dualism with bipolar emotions. What I mean by this, is that once we experience something emotional in a past event, we tend to have positive or negative emotion, and be affected or controlled by the event.

But, once we experience love and gratitude for the same event in the recognition of a world of transformation, as Lynn did, the past event appears with empowerment in front of us now and here. Yes. As Lynn and Dr J F Demartini said, "Nothing is missing in the Universe" and "There is nothing but love. All else is illusion." This book gives us very important chances for us to awaken to true love and gratitude that exist now and here, and have empowering experiences beyond time and space.

I personally "lost" my ex-girlfriend and I felt her love and gratitude when I saw her in different forms in my life. Her death brought me great opportunities to explore the human mind on a very deep level—it opened my new life. I understand "loss" always comes with "gain" in some forms. I felt as if I met not only Lynn's sisters but also my ex-girlfriend while I was reading this book. Thank you, Lynn.

My country, Japan has been experiencing a great amount of "loss" since the big earthquake and tsunami hit Japan in March 11, 2011. It is said that around 15,000people "lost" their lives because of the event. The families and friends who "lost" their loved ones are still being bowed by grief I really want them to find "new gain" in their lives from the bottom of my heart to empower their lives. I do believe that this book will be one of the most empowering books for those who lost their loved ones due to the event. One day, I do hope that Japanese people will read this book and find their new life opportunities to contribute to rebuilding the country. Love and Gratitude."

Tsunehiro Nonaka

"For the past seven years I have been grieving and missing my parents: they passed away one month apart from one another. At the time of their passing, I had two young babies and for them I had to push through the pain. The grief became more apparent as my children would get older. Every day I would wish my parents were alive to see my children grow. In April this year I was fortunate to attend and participate in a seminar The Breakthrough Experience®. During the weekend, Dr J F Demartini took me through Side C of The Demartini Method®—a tool designed to dissolve loss and grief. At the beginning and during of the process I was very emotional and sceptical. At the end of the process I was so grateful to have been a part of it. The process helped me realize that I actually see my parent's everyday through my children, family and friends. Now when I think of my parents all I can do is smile. I now do not fear loss anymore and I am grief free."

Adriana Virgo, Perth

"As a fellow Facilitator in The Demartini Method®, I am truly blessed to have met Lynn Hope Thomas. Lynn's capacity to open her heart to love is immense. I am in awe of her willingness to lay bare her life, so that she can help others to truly find unconditional love, something that she has most definitely assisted me in doing. I am honoured to share this amazing and profound transformational method with Lynn, and deeply grateful to call her my friend."

Laura Mullens, Facilitator in The Demartini Method®

"Having experienced loss and grief when at the age of 19, and three weeks after leaving home, my mum past away, I spent the next 27 years trying to understand and come to terms with the impact that this had on my life, how unfair life had been, and also the guilt I carried. It was when I discovered Dr. John Demartini, and The Demartini Method®, that Ifinally understood, and let go of the guilt I carried, It is with sincere gratitude to Lynn for her courage and dedication

to write this book for you, and I trust that through reading this book you will live a more fulfilling life. Thank you, Lynn."

Kate Brain, Facilitator in The Demartini Method®

"Before meeting Lynn, a great facilitator in The Demartini Method®, I knew there were the seeds of change in my life, but could not see with the clarity that I have now. I had no idea that the events and people of my past could be gifts to me. I thought that losing my ex-girlfriend as a direct result of my own self-loathing and her moving away from the UK to Australia was one of the lowest and most negative experiences. It transpires that this was a guide to a wake-up call that to myself to travel halfway round the world for love, I didn't get the love of my girlfriend back, instead the realisation of the love for myself and now thanks to Lynn's help a new sense of balance and synchronicity in life' that I intend to build on."

Hugo Fitzjohn, United Kingdom

Even though I attended The Breakthrough Experience couple of times, working with issues isn't always easy. Lynn's book helped me to see loss in a different light and made me realize issues in my own life. I was able to deal with them and turn them into blessings.

Sometimes it is convenient to pity yourself but there are times when even we get sick of it. At those times you want to have Lynn's book available to help you deal with loss and get over it in matter of hours, rather than years. Highly recommended.

Juraj Benak, IT professional, Brisbane

Life has always been fraught with its twists and turns. Always does it provide us with opportunities to either soar in spirit or feel the soreness in failing to optimize the best in our circumstances. The powerful book, "Breaking Through Loss", has been able to capture what it means to feel the absence of loved ones and through it all, develop the courage and strength to live for those we cherish the most and carry on the legacies of those we can see no more.

My Friend and a mentor, Lynn Hope Thomas, has faced the worse that could happen to anyone. Having lost her sisters to death at a young age and exposed to psychological and emotional traumas, she has been able to take responsibility for her life and take charge of her circumstances.

No one can better explain the journey from pain to pleasure, sadness to joy and weakness to strength, than one who has had to endure a predicament beyond what she could cure at a point in time. Her book, "Breaking through Loss" is indeed revealing and soul inspiring as she has been able to provide the world with what it entails to overcome emotional and psychological traumas and indeed break through loss.

Having gained the opportunity to explore Lynn Hope Thomas' world in the little time I have come to know her and by reading her book, I have had cause to shape my thoughts and develop positive attitudes to life, as it turns out to be the one paramount factor that has brought her this far in life.

Lynn Hope Thomas is a rare treasure and one of the best things that have happened in this generation. She is a source of inspiration and a blessing to many. To me as a person and as a friend, she is a priceless gift and I can only imagine how lucky and glad her families would be to have her in their lives.

I have no doubt in mind that her maiden book, "Breaking through Loss", is a stepping stone to her greatness. Lynn Hope Thomas is fulfilling her destiny and she is just a step away from making a remarkable difference in this cruel and bitter sweet world of ours.

You can achieve as much as she has achieved as well, as long as you are willing and ready to adapt to change, give in to positivity and adopt the methods she has used over time to break through the shackles of depression and dejection.

I hope the astonishing messages in this book reach deep down to the heart of those who can afford to get a copy and change their lives for the better. If Lynn can break through her loss to living the better life, what stops you from experiencing the feel of happiness, contentment and living with a purpose? God bless you Lynn! I admire you and am highly privileged and honoured to have you as a friend."

Jacobs Adewale, Mass Communications Expert, Lagos

"As a fellow facilitator who has inspired and been inspired by Lynn, she is a fabulous example of the science of transformation using The Demartini Method® at work. When we understand what our Universe truly is and our role in it I am truly humbled by the power we have in ourselves, and the ability to awaken this in our fellow beings with the Demartini Method. Applying this method with loss in very recent months with the sudden passing of my father has been a true test for me, I am forever grateful as myself and my family get to appreciate Tom even more as we realise that energy cannot be created or destroyed, it's transformed. We see real evidence his essence and energy are all around us. In the words of my

16 year old daughter, she feels that the grief has been transformed or replaced with appreciation. Instead of reality we are seeing actuality. Thank you, Lynn for bringing this book out to help heal and transform people by dissolving their grief and loss using The Demartini Method®, and for sharing your journey with us."

Mandy Beverley, RGON, Auckland, New Zealand

"I have worked with many highly knowledgeable and experienced facilitators from those who charge $50 an hour, to $6000 for the day, up to $2200 per hour. However what makes Lynn stand out is she has that key essential element of an open heart and a genuine love of people."

**David W Burch—Business Owner, Author,
and Investor, Perth, Australia**

"I had a private consult with Lynn regarding a relationship issue. Lynn made me feel at ease instantly and quickly pinpointed my issue. Then, using The Demartini Method®, she worked through the columns and dissolved it until I could only feel love and gratitude. I felt a huge burden had lifted. Thank you, Lynn."

Debora Spencer, Gladstone Qld

"Lynn Hope Thomas has an amazing ability to make you feel comfortable around her and open up about the "pains"you have going on in your life and assists you to break through these using the Demartini Method. It's an amazing journey that you experience when you are working on dissolving all the issues that you have in your life. Thank you Lynn for being the amazing and loving person that you are."

Ala Almaet, Teckhead Solutions, Sydney, Australia

"It has been an honour to work with Lynn in writing her first published book, Breaking Through Loss. Having been a student and facilitator in Dr. John Demartini's work for nearly six years now, I understand deeply how the methodology Lynn writes about—The Demartini Method®—has incredible power to transform lives as it has also done to mine. Finding my calling as an Author, Speaker and Mentor, I have now worked with several high profile individuals in book writing and mentoring. Time and time again I am inspired by the amazing stories that I hear—and Lynn's is no exception.

I have been inspired many times by Lynn's sheer persistence, dedication and inspiration for this book. But more than that, I've been touched by the same persistence, dedication and inspiration that Lynn has for her clients. She sees people's need to break free from the emotions of grief and loss, no matter what area of life they are experiencing them in or over. She has the strength and the drive to push people through to their own freedom—the ability to move on and create an amazing life. I recommend this book for anyone who knows it's time to change, transform and get on with their life' and balance the emotions of the past, to live in the beautiful present, as nothing is ever truly missing."

**Emily Gowor, The Word Artist—
Best-selling Author, Speaker and Mentor**

"In the bare truth of vulnerability lies great power. This book is a courageous, heart-warming and truly inspirational account of one Woman's journey through chaotic loss and the invaluable lessons of growth as she discovers order and eternal love in the Universe."

Calina Ouliaris, Mindset Consultant

"As a fellow Student of Life and practitioner who utilizes 'The Demartini Method'—the tool with a 1000 uses for empowering life, I highly commend Lynn for her dedication to not only using the method to transform her own life, but too also her dedication, commitment and her astuteness to employ her own unique approach to The Demartini Method® to achieve maximum results in dealing with, grief sorrow, bereavement and loss. Well done Lynn, may you transform the lives of those who are ready to receive the gift of your services.

Michael Brown, Perth

"As a fellow facilitator and helping others through their grief and loss I never knew how it really felt, until two weeks ago when I lost my dear dad. I took my self through the method as soon as I heard the news, and sure enough the pain in my heart was gone, no feeling off loss or grief at all, just a few tears of love and gratitude, knowing that he will always be in my heart."

Don Aylett, Mudgee Western N.S.W

FOREWORD

Can human beings truly and permanently transform their crises into blessings, their challenges into opportunities and their scars into stars simply through changing their perceptions, interpretations and attitudes? The answer is emphatically...yes!

Lynn Hope Thomas has certainly done so in her own life and has now helped many others do exactly the same with theirs. But how, you may ask, could she have actually achieved such meaningful and lasting transformations? Through learning and practically applying a unique human transformational methodology called the *Demartini Method*® which she was introduced to while she attended one of my signature seminar programs, titled *The Breakthrough Experience*® just a few years ago.

If you are picking up this book to read, then it's a sign that you are probably looking for some inspiring new way to help you through what may be a challenging period in your life—or help someone else's life you also truly care about. Through the chapters, Lynn demonstrates in a heartfelt recount of her personal life events, the impact that burying our unresolved emotions has on our lives, minds and bodies. I feel certain that this autobiography will provide you with insight into how you may dissolve any remaining perceptions of undissolved grief from loss in a touching and personal way that is effective, authentic and from the heart.

After reading the extreme impact that perceptions of grief had on Lynn's relationships and career, you will realise how significant the *Demartini*

Method® has been in bringing Lynn to the awakening that the apparently challenging events of her life were actually **'on the way'**, and not **in the way**.

Part of this powerful, scientific methodology explains and demonstrates how nothing is ever actually missing—it only exists in an unrecognized and ever changing form. As there are no challenges without opportunities, no step backs without step forwards, no scars without stars, and no losses without gains, this method can help you transform yourself from being a victim of your history to a master of your destiny, because masters live in the world of transformation, not in the illusive world of gain and loss.

As one of my trained Facilitators in the *Demartini Method*®, Lynn Hope Thomas experienced the perception of extraordinary grief first-hand in more than one area of her life before discovering the method that has initially brought and continues to bring meaningful transformations to her life. This book is a testament to that.

When I was in the first grade, I was told by my first grade teacher that I would never be able to read, write or communicate, never amount to anything and never go very far in life. For ten years, I believed it. I dropped out of school at age fourteen and pan-handled as a bum on the streets. At age seventeen, after coming close to dying, I met an inspiring teacher named Paul C. Bragg who believed that I was capable of activating a hidden genius and awakening and applying an inner wisdom that I was unaware I had. His clarity transformed my awareness of myself and my destiny. I suddenly believed that I too, through learning, could help others transform their lives.

Since then I have dedicated the last 40 years of my life to researching and understanding human behaviour and originating a reproducible scientific method—the *Demartini Method*®—to help people to break through their trying emotional challenges that hold them back from living inspired and magnificent lives. The *Demartini Method*® is now being facilitated in over 60 countries throughout the world by psychiatrists, psychologists, therapists, other health professionals, consultants, coaches, business leaders etc… and I now have a few thousand Facilitators worldwide who have been professionally-trained to share and facilitate the method for people of all walks of life.

As a *Demartini Method*® facilitator, Lynn has worked relentlessly to pursue her dream of transforming people's lives that have lived through similar perceived adversities and it is meaningful to me to see people get up onto their own two feet again and in turn contribute something magnificent to the world as a result of her efforts. I have watched Lynn continue to be a catalyst in the transformation of other people's lives and assist them in dissolving their perceptions of grief and loss that had previously stopped them from moving on and appreciating and loving their lives.

It is deeply inspiring to me to think that because of my life's study and dedication to developing a reproducible science, Lynn has devoted her life to offering a great example of overcoming adversity using my method and I know that Lynn's story will add to the thousands of people around the world who are being freed from their emotional challenges and scars and released to go on and do something truly meaningful and inspirational in the world.

Love and Wisdom

Dr. John F. Demartini

Founder of the Demartini Institute

www.DrDemartini.com

INTRODUCTION

I never imagined that one day I would write a book, let alone decide that I had a more books inside of me. During the writing of this autobiographical book *(Breaking Through Loss: One Powerful Story, One Scientific Method)*, I witnessed some of Australia's worst floods in history, an inland tsunami, and a Category 5 cyclone, not to mention the earthquakes that have hit Christchurch and then the great tsunami and knock-on nuclear disaster in Japan. It seems uncanny, and yet the message that hits home for me is that I have a very worthy story to tell which will be received by many of the people experiencing loss of some kind, and by those who feel they keep repeating the trauma of loss.

The first 40 years of my life have been affected by repeated loss and perceived painful circumstances causing what felt like no end of sadness. I kept the lid tightly closed on all the pain, sadness and anger that I felt inside—after all, who wants to hear your emotional story? Isn't it the 'right' thing to do to put a brave face on and realise that others have it worse? And yet, at times it doesn't feel like the right thing to do. Well, in my 40 years of experience it is precisely the wrong thing to do and it sets you up for further grief until you allow yourself to experience the flow of the emotions.

This is my story. It is personal and it takes all my energy and courage to reveal it to you. I would not do it normally but I do it because I had the pleasure of listening to a remarkable gentleman called Dr. John Demartini. Everything he said made total sense to me. It was like I had waited all my life to hear him. Everything he spoke of was true and the truth.

For the first time in my life I felt awakened and wanting to know more about the truth.

How can I say that? Well, once you discover the truth there is no turning back. My life suddenly made the most sense it had ever made. Imagine searching for decades, and then finally what you are looking for is revealed to you. It's an amazing discovery and I want to share it with you. It may take me a little time but first you need to understand what has been happening in my life.

This book will demonstrate beyond doubt that the Universe will encourage and then force you to address your issues, and until you do, the power and intensity will increase until you listen. Let me repeat that: My book will demonstrate beyond doubt that the Universe will force you to address your issues and until you do, the power and intensity of the challenges in your life will increase until you listen—and wake up to the presence of a power greater than yourself. I don't make this statement lightly. I want you to dwell on it and allow the thought to etch in your mind. For if you should experience loss and feel you have dealt with it, and then some other tragedy or loss happens, I want you to remember and recall what I have said. This book will lead you back to the only scientific method of all that will allow you to truly and genuinely move on with your life.

This book aims to enlighten people about the wonderful and relatively speedy method of self-discovery called The Demartini Method®—the tool with 1000 uses for empowering life. It can be used for loss and grief or for any other reoccurring human emotion or event that is running your life. You can free yourself up to live the life that you deserve.

The Demartini Method® is the life's work of Dr. John Demartini—a well-respected Human Behaviour Specialist, international best-selling Author of multiple books and a prolific Speaker who has developed a science to human behaviour. After discovering Dr J F Demartini's profound and transformational body of work and experiencing the way in which the application of The Demartini Method® completely resolved my biggest life challenges in a matter of hours, I realised it was my purpose in life to offer support to people to help them resolve their unnecessary suffering. And yes, suffering is absolutely unnecessary.

This book—*Breaking Through Loss*—is the first that shows deep loss and grief, recurring over a span of 40 years and then gives a real, authentic account of what happened after attending The Breakthrough Experience® with Dr J F Demartini. It also gives numerous accounts of the insights and wonders that continuing to apply the method brings—all of which were recorded during the writing of this book and can be found in the *Appendix*. In *Chapter 12: Time For You To Love Loss,* this book shows you exactly how you too can bring results to your own life and determine the life you want to live as opposed to feeling that events and outside circumstances are running your life.

I am amazed at how much emotional pain the human being can tolerate—I have had a large dose of it over the years of my own life. I am not unique here: many people suffer in their emotions and many of them have different ways of handling their emotions and feeling of grief. I am respectful of those choices. For those who can no longer tolerate the impact of loss—then I am here to help them. It's my personal mission to bring them forward with a leading edge and exciting tool that dissolves the issue of loss. It has the power to empower one's life in one of seven key areas: spiritually, mentally, vocationally, financially, within the family, socially and physically.

Put quite simply, this mission is my mission from God. It is my purpose and soul being, and I know in my heart it is the truth. I am rock-solid on this and cannot be moved. It feels wonderful and also liberating, to finally "come out" of my shell and speak out from the soul. This can sometimes take tremendous courage, and this book will unleash the same fire and courage from within you. I feel like I am heading home (at last) after a long journey that has spanned 40 years. It was not that I hadn't sought any help or read any self-help books either; I had read plenty along the way. Somehow, some way the Universe wanted to get me to continue my journey all the way to Australia and search for answers that could explain my life's apparent mishaps. I discovered The Demartini Method® and I knew instantly that my life would never be the same again.

The Demartini Method® is a breakthrough discovery and cuttingedge personal transformation methodology which results in a new perspective and paradigm in thinking and feeling. It is the culmination of more than 40 years of research and studies by Dr J F Demartini in numerous disciplines including physics, philosophy, theology, metaphysics, psychology, astronomy, mathematics, neurology and physiology. The method can be applied to many situations and is for anyone who wants to overcome strong and dominant emotions over any life event. There are several 'sides' to The Demartini Method® and each one can be applied to dissolve different emotions in a range of circumstances. The primary sides of the method (which are being used in several countries on thousands of people worldwide) are Side A, Side B and Side C. This book will explore the power of Side C as it is relevant to dissolving loss and grief. The method may not be everyone's 'cup of tea' but there is absolutely no denying that the scientific method works when you work it. This has been witnessed by many thousands and the numbers are growing. I truly believe that one day this method will be part of the education of our children.

We all have different missions in life. God let us choose this way. Some have a defined purpose and that might not be to discover profound insights. It might be that you have a lesser academic yearning and your fulfilment is, for example, to bring smiles to the faces of people. This life purpose is of equal importance and designed equally to deliver profound messages to intelligent beings. We are all equal in the eyes of God. There is not one being that is more supreme than any other. Equality is, just as God's love is.

I believe its the book brings *authentic results* for the simple reason that it means that once you have dealt with your issues, then they are dissolved completely—transformed—and you won't have to face them again, like I did. It does not mean that you can avoid loss, it's a natural part of life and we all encounter loss, again and again. Only after reading this book will you learn that you can change the form in which you experience loss, and you can embrace it for all of its goodness and treasures. It may be hard for many people to imagine feeling like this when they have lost the dearest of persons—someone who they felt was their closest love and their world and purpose. My life record has been about the repetitive nature of some of these things and I want you to see firsthand, from my experience, what can happen if you don't adequately deal with the issues. I also know it is not that easy at times to identify the issue.

This is another key point about The Demartini Method® and how powerful it is: You do become more aware of when an issue is arising. As you become more aware, you can then do something about it and take action on what you have emotions about. Otherwise, guaranteed, it will pop up somewhere else in your life as a recurring theme until it is put to bed and you truly see and experience the divine perfection of your life.

Writing this book has been like swimming lengths of the pool for an hour. At first it's a daunting long-haul, and then as you start to get to the midway point it begins to speed up and finally you get into the home run, which feels good. As I write my book my journey and progress unfolds, I receive enlightenment along the way. I receive encouragement from leaders and guides who are willing me on. I am grateful for their help. This really is the start of my authentic life journey and it feels very different to my earlier life but I could not have reached this point if I hadn't travelled here so I am equally grateful to everything in my earlier life that has brought me here and now.

Life is like looking at a movie: The viewer always remains the same at any given moment, but what has past has gone and what is ahead we don't know. We can only live and be in the present. Thank you for the precious present, it is indeed the most authentic moment one can experience in life. I hope that you enjoy reading about my life story, and more than this, I hope that it touches a chord and that you can recognise the beauty of what I want to share. Enjoy reading about the subsequent changes that followed on in my life after The Breakthrough Experience® and from using The Demartini Method® in my life on a regular basis. I hope that it will inspire you to reflect on your own situation and unresolved emotions and then seek out authentic help that will take you from where you are to where you would love to be.

For me, I wish to continue my healing and so too share my experience with you. In doing so, I will teach you that you too can begin to heal your life. That's why I thought I would capture some key events for me during the process of this healing and these can be found in the Appendix. I know listening to another's story can assist in understanding the process for some people and allow them to understand what can happen when one begins the authentic journey to understanding one's soul.

In the book I have changed the names of individuals to protect their privacy. It is important to understand that my perceptions of situations and other's actions have created my nightmares, and my losses. It is my created journey as I learn to love myself and to navigate through life.

I am truly grateful for all of my relationships and the truth of love as they have reflected and do reflect to me, the parts I was disowning. It is an honour to me that they played a beautiful and loving part in my life. It is this revolutionary scientific method that has woken me up to my own creations of how I am here to help enlighten others.

CHAPTER 1

Innocent Days

"In their innocence, very young children know themselves to be light and love. If we will allow them, they can teach us to see ourselves the same way."
Michael Jackson

I grew up in a beautiful little village called Rodington in the heart of the Shropshire countryside in England. My parents, Bill and Jean Hope Thomas, were married at the tender age of 18 years old and they are still together today, some 60 years later. Their firstborn children were identical twins named Janet and Hazel Hope Thomas. I love saying their names—it reminds me that they are in my heart forever. I always think it was an amazing fact that they were my two sisters and those sisters were two years, two months and two days older than me. I use the number two as my lucky number sometimes. It reminds me that there are signs and clues of the divine all around us in the world, if only we are open to seeing them.

We had what can only be described as a blissful childhood; playing on farms with a variety of farm animals. It was fun to jump onto the roofs of corrugated iron pig sheds and tease the pigs. We would collect the eggs from the chicken houses; in fact we would spend a fair bit of time with the lovely hens and baking mud pies in the sun. Being in the countryside, we could exercise on our bicycles; a favourite was to cycle up Haughmond

Hill and freewheel down the long hill that was some three kilometres in length. Some days our bicycles would be treated as if they were horses and we would groom them carefully. Believing they were horses like this was the only time they ever got cleaned.

At other times the bikes would be turned into motorbikes, by clipping cardboard to the wheel spokes with Mum's pegs for the washing line. We had total freedom to roam, climb trees, and befriend all of nature's creatures. The creatures ranged from horses, cows, and pigs to baby partridges and bunnies that were rescued from the fields before the farmer almost ploughed them away. As sisters we were intimately close. I was continually competing in order to keep up with them. If they played the piano, I could play. If they played chess, I could play. I loved playing, I loved the adventures and I loved them being in my life.

We all went to High Ercall Primary school. It was the sweetest village school with a wonderful Headmistress called Mrs Taylor. The twins looked so alike that they, naturally, would sometimes play tricks on people, pretending to be each other and creating all kinds of chaos for other people to figure out. The funny thing was that to us in our family they looked very different. We could see the differences in their appearance and in their personalities that others who weren't so close weren't able to see. Here is a photograph, have a look and see what you think:

Mum and Dad were proud of all us all. At the sports day in the village, we would all compete, running and winning most of the races… or at least it felt like that to us, as we enjoyed it so thoroughly. The prize money was excellent, and we would go and hand over the money to Mum. That would inevitably create even more great memories. Something I notice today is that memories seem to get rosier and rosier as I get older. The things that once challenged me now seem so trivial when I look back on my past and I appreciate the experiences I have had. I know this is true for so many other people too. We can so easily forget all the bad days, arguments and fights. We do need to be careful though, because ignoring the balancing traits can set us up for an addiction which leads to grief and, as you will learn in the book that leads to potentially extreme consequences.

My mum often dressed us in identical outfits. She knitted cardigans and jumpers and even made dresses for us. We became known as the "Beverly Sisters" after the famous triplets, purely because people believed we were triplets. I'll admit it—I loved it and I definitely loved the attention. People loved to look at us. For us, it meant we often got ice-creams and sweets unexpectedly from strangers. These were rare treats in those days. I must say I am grateful to those people who created these memories for me. It would seem like they knew to create them for me.

You might think that sounds slightly crazy—and perhaps it is. It's a part of me that I own and love very dearly, for it was my craziness that carried me through the many perceived traumas in my life, and that also gave me a balance to actually keep me sane.

I was six years old when Mum and Dad bought us a lovely Golden Retriever puppy. She was so athletic. We trained her to jump high walls and fences—she was brilliant. I trained her to walk up planks of wood, carry eggs in her mouth without breaking them, and she could easily track any scent by sniffing. Dad used her as a gun dog and it made us laugh to hear that she would find the bird he had shot but then he would have to find the dog and the bird because she would not pick the bird up. Clever girl! We all had an aversion to death and we all so loved animals. Someone said to me just last month that she believed dogs were created by God as companions for those without friends. I'm not sure why anyone would think that. I think there was an even bigger reason God created them. You will see later in this chapter just how much my dog meant to me. Other people say that 'Dog' is God backwards. Actually all my dogs are Gods; they give so much unconditional love for so little in return. I would love for every child to experience the pleasure of looking after a dog and all the rewards and experiences it brings.

Janet was a pure genius. She continually came up with fantastic ideas and was the more serious of the twins, whereas Hazel was more jolly and silly, and she liked to have as much fun as possible. Hazel was also very clever in her studies. She was only one point behind Janet in her school tests for secondary school. There are many stories of the genius that both of my sisters showed in their lives.

Janet and Hazel had me collect wood and, with Dad's saws and some nails, Janet began making an aeroplane that meant we could fly home. She did not want us to get off the school bus and have to walk a mile home. Now with my daughter Lauren who is ten years old as I write, I remain in awe at the brilliance of children to do great things with their imagination and their creativity.

Janet was eight years old at the time and I was six. I knew it was going to work—talk about excitement. I couldn't wait for it to be finished. Clearly, I too hated walking a mile home, but there was another factor embedded here. It was the genius of Janet who saw no restriction on what we could do, as children, to solve our problems. Janet's seed was planted in me, and that is the seed I would love to grow for the future, for the sake of two wonderful twins, for the life I have lived and for making it all count for something.

Janet was ready to do it—to take off and fly—yet for some reason it has taken me nearly 50 years to truly do it in my own life. That's okay, and I understand the divine timing that is at play here in the world: I would not wish to give you something that was not ready for worthiness before its time. Christmas time was approaching and we were getting excited at the prospect of presents, just as children do. We were artists at climbing the cupboards and finding the gifts that were hidden away. Mum never knew but we would unwrap and rewrap our spoilt surprises. Though, I must say it never took the excitement or the specialness of Christmas Day away from us. It was like two Christmases in one. We would take it in turns to stay awake with a book and a torch. And yes, guess who would always fall asleep—yours truly—I was reliably unreliable. What we didn't know at the time, as our excitement continued to build, was that this Christmas was going to be different, just simply not the same as in previous years.

We were playing in the lounge when Hazel suddenly started screaming and covering her own ears. She was in physical agony and there wasn't anything that we could do to comfort her. Stricken with concern, the whole family piled into the car and we all went off to the hospital for "tests". I don't know what they were testing for but, as we were sisters and closely related, the hospital was convinced that we all needed to be checked. Janet and Hazel got taken in for more "tests" and I was sent home as being "okay"—yet somehow, nothing felt okay about it at all. Why couldn't I have the same attention? What was happening? I was completely miffed.

The twins' illness progressed and they were taken to the Birmingham Children's Hospital which was a two hour journey from our house—it was a real haul for my two, deeply worried parents. And, of course, this hospital was the Midlands equivalent of Great Ormond street of London—where only the very sick children are sent. Not that I knew that at the age of nine. Perhaps it was a blessing in disguise in hindsight. I recall visiting once, maybe twice but I also recall moaning about how long we were spending there. I also recall the subsequent guilt I felt about my behaviour…however, had I been told they were dying, I wouldn't have moaned. I would have told them how much I loved them, my two sweet darling sisters.

And so, Christmas that year was no fun at all for anyone. Janet and Hazel were in the hospital and Mum and Dad were at the hospital. Janet and Hazel's presents lay unopened under the tree on Christmas Day; some were never to be opened by them. I was at home and my Nanna was with us. She had clearly been invited down to help look after me. I wasn't really sure what to do with my time during those days. Sometimes I would stay at my friend's house and have a great time and a ball, little knowing that my sisters were fading away fast. It seems like my pleasure was in absolute contrast to the pain and suffering that both of my parents were going through. I couldn't even see it in their faces, nor see the amount of weight my father had lost. It was in subsequent years that a neighbour recalled the change in him, she told me how "gaunt" he had looked; indeed a "different man".

One day Dad was quietly talking to Nanna in another room, when their silent muffled talk made my ears prick up. I remember hearing a shriek escape from Nanna. I couldn't tell if she was laughing or crying. I had a 'sense,' a fear, a moment of immense intuition. I began to cry, something terrible had definitely happened to my sister. As Dad came through to me in the next room, he asked why I was crying. I suddenly felt very stupid, afraid of the answer to the question, yet I wanted to be stupid, crying for nothing, because nothing had happened. Oh but it had. I rushed over to him and he put his arms around me and confirmed the horror to me that Hazel had died.

'God, what! Hazel, how? How could that be? My sister! Thank God for Janet!'

Some saving grace had blessed us. These were my thoughts in that moment, even as a child, so I said to Nanna, "Don't cry, at least we have Janet left." She scolded me; it hurt. It's only now that I can comprehend why it appeared as such an insensitive thing to say. I was only nine years old, and now I only have to look at my lovely daughter Lauren to comprehend the thinking of a child at that age. I recall Hazel's funeral at the village church. I was embarrassed to cry in public and I didn't want anyone to see my pain, so I dug my nails into my palms to stop me from crying. I looked at school friends and their parents, and they were all crying, so I refused to cry. It was very hard to do that—I pushed and pushed the pain inwards. My nails were beginning to draw blood from my hand, so I squeezed tighter. I learned that pain goes away, at least temporarily, once it gets too much. "Why?" I asked myself, "are they crying? It's not *their* sister; it's my sister who died. They have no idea of the pain, the loss. Would I really want them to?"

The thoughts ran through my head. I wanted to see her; I wanted to hug her for just one last time, Hazel! What would people think if I ran to the coffin and opened it up? I can't do that, but I *do* want to do that, I want to see her, she can't be dead…she can't! I was silent on the outside, but on the inside the scream of pain tore a hollow space in me.

The cremation brought no relief. Curtains closed around the coffin as it was being lowered and then the curtains opened again. I could still see the coffin being lowered. I remember thinking that they were a bit quick with opening the curtains. I knew what was going to happen to the coffin. My heart sank—she was to be burnt now and gone forever. It all seemed so final. Yet, somehow it was and somehow it wasn't. The mark it left on me appeared to be forever and it's only as I work through The Demartini Method® in my life today (the tool I will introduce you to in the upcoming chapters of this book) that I can heal the wounds that Hazel's and Janet's passing appeared to have left in my body. I also come to this later in my book about how it is remarkable that grief can be gone forever following a series of questions aligned to this scientific method.

After Hazel's funeral, my mum told me that Janet was coming home for the weekend and this was a great joy to my ears. My sister was coming home, how good was that! I wanted to skip and dance and sing out loud. It seemed so much like a silver lining after a dark cloud had covered the sunny skies.

Janet first came on the Friday to visit her friends at the primary school. The school was joyful and everyone was so pleased to see Janet. I remember that Mrs Taylor went round with a basket of chocolates for all the children. To this day I bless her for that, she created a memory that is so beautiful. Yet I have another memory too, of how frail Janet was—her tiny wrists were almost pure bone, and she looked like a child, starving and suffering from malnutrition. Her frailty brought a lump to my throat. Yet it was as if my sister had wholeness to her, one that the extreme frailty could not take away. Janet was Janet, it was her beautiful spirit that shone and it was more than her physical being. She was glad to see her friends and it was lovely to see her smile even though the weakness of her body was evident on that day…it's a miracle she made it to school at all.

My parents took us for a trip to one of Janet's favourite beauty spots, the hills in Church Stretton, Shropshire. As kids, this was the equivalent of a white knuckle ride. Cars would have to pass on narrow roads, and there was always the potential that we would fall over the cliff edge. The thought was always at the forefront of our minds…it was frightening and scary but we loved it. I guess I believed then that Janet was better and that we would spend the day as a normal one. It wasn't to be, however. She was so tired, so I let her place her head on my lap and she slept peacefully.

I recall feeling really "saintly" for having allowed her to do this…I was such an impatient creature at times. My Nanna always said that patience was a virtue and I can really thank Janet now for giving me this opportunity to feel like that in that moment. Indeed, there are many messages and communications that were given to me, and as I unravel each of them I realise the full glory of my sisters lives and what their mission on earth was to accomplish, as well as my own mission.

My parents were doing what they thought was best, so they didn't tell me about the impending truth that was coming. It was like I had it set in my mind that at least Janet was alive…that was until the morning when I saw Mum enter the Headmistress's office. Once again that same strong intuition made me scream inside…

CHAPTER 2

Doctrine Of Double Effect

"The doctrine (or principle) of double effect is often invoked to explain the permissibility of an action that causes a serious harm, such as the death of a human being, as a side effect of promoting some good end."

Author Unknown

"No!!!"

It was like a sledgehammer hitting my brain. Every cell in my body was in trauma. Mum emerged from the Headmistress's office, and came over to me and said, "Come on Lynn, we are going up to Nanna's". She didn't really have to say anything because I already knew what had happened yet inside, my ego kept saying this is all a big joke, it's not happening. It was so unreal. It was so far-fetched. You can't just lose sisters like that... can you? There had to be another explanation; it must be some bizarre, twisted, cruel joke. I thought that was it, that everything was really okay, and someone just wanted to tease me. Yet as I looked at Mum's face the pain of loss was written in her eyes, the truth could be seen there. My sister was dead.

When we arrived at Nanna's place, all the family were coming and going. I felt like I was in a *Tom and Jerry* cartoon. I never saw their faces

I only heard their voices, no-one touched me or spoke directly to me, they just looked at me, cried and said, "Poor girl". There was very little realisation back then about grief, and in particular how to comfort or assist a grieving child. So, in the space of one short month, I had lost both my beautiful and wonderful sisters and entered the raw world of grief. Thus began an imbalance that was to span the next 40 years of my life.

My life changed instantly. In many respects it was a good thing that my mother had let me go to church each week. In a lot of ways, I've known throughout my life that God is there—Church isn't the only place where God can be reached or contacted. I have been having a conversation with God for a great part of my life.

This is the point where my relationship with God really took off. The questions I needed to ask, the answers I was looking for. *Why them? Why not me? Who made them die? Did someone kill them? Was it my grandmother?* It was a bizarre twist of my mind, but I thought it was my grandmother because I was given the watch she had bought for Janet and Hazel. I figured out at age nine that she must have killed them so that I could have the watch. I knew it had to be wrong, because someone would have figured out it that was murder and they hadn't. There were no detectives coming to our house. I watched in hope every day to find an answer to why this trauma was occurring.

I placed all my trust in God, absolutely. The Bible says that if you believe strongly enough and your faith is unwavering, then all things are possible. I latched onto that thought, by heck! I didn't let it go, even for one brief second or moment in time. It was exactly what I needed to get me through my trauma, and through the first, extreme challenge of my life.

No-one, not even my parents, were talking to me about the ordeal. They just let it go silently, as though there was nothing to be said about it now that both Janet and Hazel had passed on. I sometimes wonder if they knew just how many burning questions I had inside my mind—questions and thoughts which were raging inside my mind about the whole event. And so, God was my first port of call and the greatest comfort in my times of need. I spent a lot of time in solitary, contemplating, looking in the pages of the Bible, and trying to find the answer. I kept on thinking, "God said if you believed enough, then all things were possible." The miracle of the woman who had died and Jesus brought her to life, meant for sure that

I could bring my sisters back. From that day forth I prayed as hard as I could. Every time we ate chicken I would wish on the chicken wishbone, and every morning I would wake up and wonder when God was going to send them back to me.

In hindsight, I did receive a message that assisted me through the emotional pain. It came in the form of the Vicar who was visiting Mum one day. I had a sick goldfish at the time, which Dad put in an old ceramic sink filled with water. Dad was treating it with some potion or other. The Vicar asked me what was wrong, and so I told him that my fish was ill. He then blessed my fish and said, "Lord, let Lynn's fish get better". As I ran out the next morning believing my fish would be ready to go back into the pond, there it was floating on top of the water. The message appeared to be that God couldn't do much about it. Still…it didn't stop me believing and trying. I quickly became an expert in hoping beyond all hope. Hoping for the impossible to become possible and for doorways to open up where many would have given up sooner.

I recall in moments of contemplation of the why and asking God for the answer I intuitively knew that there was a reason, all was not in my awareness and to trust in God.

Fortunately I was able to focus on my physical strengths and this helped to distract from the grief. The exercise and goals I set for myself became my greatest source of comfort. I was a practicing gymnast and this required focus and mental attention as well as allowing my body to dance and move to music. I could so totally lose myself in the workout. I also played a lot of tennis at the High Ercall tennis club and recall the delight of Mum and Dad when I won the junior championship. They laughed when I complained that I wanted the second prize of sweets and not the silver cup as a reward for my efforts. I really believe that a lot of my repressed grief and sorrow was released in sport and movement. I am so grateful for this, having met many other people whose repressed emotions have resulted in body illnesses and cancers.

As I mentioned earlier, my dog played a very important role for me during my childhood. Her name was Cally, she gave me the second greatest comfort. It was Cally who became my greatest companion for the initial period of grief after my sisters passed away. Friends did not know what to say or how to comfort, but Cally knew. God gave us pets to nurse us and comfort us when we are sad. It was a different story at school. I was teased by David Straw. "You should be six feet under, with your sisters!" he shouted. How cruel can someone be? It hurt and it cut deep, but I put my brave face on, and I swallowed back the desire to cry and show my pain in front of other people. This cruelty, a part of me that I had disowned, was to rear its ugly head again and again, as was the loss, and as were the tears I refused to cry for my sisters. Until I could own the parts disowned, the Universe was going to keep bringing them back again and again.

On a lighter note, I spent a lot of time playing with my childhood friend Amanda; we crafted together making candles and making plastic moulds. We played ball, climbed trees, made dens, we practiced our gymnastics but most of all we laughed and giggled all the time. The kitchen window was our audience and we would explain to the viewer's how to make candles. It invariably would result in us laughing at our mistakes and errors in front of the audience. When I say laugh, I mean we would double up and be rolling on the floor, speechless. I recall one of my mother's friends referring to me as "the girl with the infectious laugh". I loved laughing, I could laugh until I cried, which seems ironic but then nature is balanced and the laughter provided me with a great relief from the grief. I even had an inclination to become a female comedian, I did so enjoy making people laugh. I still do.

You have now read the story of my earliest adversity in life—of how I 'lost' both of my twin sisters, my closest friends—and my first experience of loss and grief. This story is ultimately the foundation for this book, and the catalyst for this book series. This story laid the roots for much of my evolution and journey that was inevitably going to unfold in my life from there on in. You will remember that in the *Introduction*, I emphasised that what we don't love, will continue to cycle through and repeat itself in our life until we love it. My unresolved emotions from early on in my life— experiencing the loss of my two sisters—planted the seeds for those themes to grow. These themes of loss and grief continued to occur throughout my life in different relationships, and in my career. It makes it increasingly clear to me, the enormous impact emotions have on a human life.

From an early age I started to suppress my emotions and learnt to put a brave face on. For some reason I felt that it was a sign of weakness to show my emotions and tell of the real feelings swirling around in my head. Of course, this suppression created events in the future of my life for the Universe to wake me up and I had to find alternative ways to handle it.

CHAPTER 3

Relief From Grief

"The deeper that sorrow carves into your being the more joy you can contain. Is not the cup that holds your wine the very cup that was burned in the potter's oven?"

Kahlil Gibran (1883–1931)

Writing the story you have just read about my loss and grief over my twin sisters was tough. It was a big challenge for me to open up and share with the world something that was so close and personal for me. In fact, when I first wrote it, I'd finished the first draft… and I promptly and accidentally deleted it. In hindsight, I realise the Universe was testing me to see if I was ready to reveal it to the public. I was—I sat down and rewrote the entire story as you've just read it. It was then that I also realised not only how much work I still had to do to truly dissolve my own challenges, but also how important it was for other people to realise that there is a way to overcome adversities like those I experienced. It indicates to you the depths that I have reached to in order to bring this story to the surface. This is literally the first time in my life—after 40 years of burying this story but never sharing it—that I have revealed what I have been storing inside for decades.

I've felt vulnerable. I've faced the fear of being ridiculed on many occasions. Now I know with certainty that ridicule is a necessary part of growth—and I welcome it. In fact, now, as this book has been published and is in your hands, I wonder how I could have waited so long to share who I am and how I discovered the trick to overcoming emotions. It brings tears to my eyes; tears of strength and inspiration. I want to move forward and reveal my 'stuff' as you might call it, so I can get on with helping you and as many people as I can. This is my mission, my life's work, without a doubt. I love to grow and I love to inspire people to grow also.

Can I ask? Do you get it? To have gone through such adversity and to come through it I know that I am stronger and more powerful than anything that has happened to me; I can fly with the wind, I can move the mountains, I can speed through space and zip round the planets before you can blink your eyes. Tears can flow and then create rivers that wash and rejuvenate and bring newness to life again. I am enthralled at the beauty of life and how precious it is. I am amazed at the depth of emotions and I know that for whatever low there is, there is also a height and for whatever height there is, there is also a low. My journey now is to bring balance, truth and light to life and to help as many others as I can to reach that point. In doing this, I feel I will be achieving what God wants me to do. Enjoy reading my story…my intention is to inspire you, as my words come from the truth of my heart, and they have been carefully and thoughtfully opened for you to read.

It's healthy for me to do this, and it will be healthy for you to do the same for yourself in your life—to really explore your own truth and dissolve the emotions that have been or are holding you back from living a truly great life. As science and understanding progresses, we learn that our thoughts and feelings undoubtedly have a great impact on our physical bodies and can lead to disease. This is especially true if we harbour sadness, anger or other emotional pains over extended periods of time, without bringing any balance to the perceptions that created the emotions in the first place. Disease is actually a feedback mechanism to let us know that we need to change our perceptions and heal ourselves by balancing our minds. The body loves us and it works in conjunction with and as part of the Universe to make sure that we focus on what we love most and do what most fulfils us—whether that's in business or our personal life. Disease is there to guide us through the symptoms to a balanced mind, before we destroy ourselves completely through ill health and cancerous deteriorations.

As I look back at David Straw's cruelty saying that I should be six feet under with my sisters, I recall my Nanna's words in my mind, "You have to be cruel to be kind." Later on in my life I utilised The Demartini Method® to shine a new light on David's comments and see them as part of the perfection of my life. What was perceived as cruel by me in that moment was in fact, a loving soul and friendly offer of support? It sounds a bit bizarre doesn't it? This will make more and more sense to you as you keep reading and turning through these pages. Once you go down the path of appreciating this leading edge tool, you do not look back. By reading this book, you will discover a new way to deal with emotions that were once hindering you and holding you back from living life to the full. And we all want to live life to the full, right?

I passed my examination to go to secondary school. I followed a family tradition of passing the 'eleven' plus, as it was called then at the age of 10. I was smart at mathematics, and perhaps I was a bit over-infatuated with that quality in myself. The twins had taken their exams just before their deaths occurred and both had passed with high scores, with one twin scoring just one point lower than the other. The number of places were limited at the grammar school, and so the education authority let only one twin go and that was Janet, the eldest. To this day, I am bemused by the decision to split the twins up. They were content with it though, and the separation didn't seem to faze them much at all.

On the day I started at the Priory Grammar School, I was kitted out in my dead sister's clothes. She had barely worn them before being taken ill. I notice now that I have an aversion to second-hand clothes; I give plenty to jumble but I'll rarely buy jumble. I now understand why—of course, it makes total sense to me, and I'm certain it does to you as well. The new school was a real challenge for me. They had "timetables" which was a brand new concept for me. I continually seemed to be in the wrong place at the wrong time, despite having a so-called timetable. The classrooms at the school had high windows, so I would have to jump up to look in and hopefully recognise someone in the class. That way, I would know where I was or should be. All these seemingly insignificant factors added to my feelings of isolation—a feeling which grew over time.

I felt very small, lost and frightened. It didn't help me when Deirdre Colson, myteacher, asked the question, "Who has or has had sisters at this school?" I put up my hand, feeling very confused as I did. I felt the adrenaline pumping all the way through my body. I felt faint.: Was she really going to ask me about my sisters? She pricked at my pain, putting her finger right on my sore spot, and I felt it choking me. I did not like her after that. I found it so insensitive to my predicament about my sisters passing. I felt resentful and angry. I also recall perceiving her correcting the way I spoke. I was giving the answer to a question which was "love". She appeared to stress that the answer to the question was "love" and in doing so I thought that she was criticising my accent; I felt another surge of emotionally-charged anger and pain. And that was how it was for me. I was in a prison of pain, topped with layers of anger at anyone who said the wrong thing, rightly or wrongly. I call it my lasagne of pain, anger, guilt, confusion, fear, despair, and loathing. I know for certain there are many other people who understand this.

The pain is like hell, raging inside of you. How, at nine years old, could this be happening? How and where could I find help? How, at nine years old, could I possibly be equipped to deal with it? I recall thinking, "Do I have to suffer this trauma? Please, please someone help me." My cries go into my body, they don't come out, they feed the nerves of my stomach, the pit. I can't even begin to tell you how I mastered it; I almost used to feel proud of my ability to control the volcano emotion…zooop! There was no emotion coming out, I was burying my feelings then boiling over them, and it was extremely repressed. Bury, bury, bury. It was so hard and yet easier to do than face the truth and the light. The brain can't take emotions but the stomach, with all its acid, can churn it all up like a washing machine. The inner cry fades amongst the noise, and it all seems like a good way of dispensing that pain or at least storing it until a later date.

On a brighter note I befriended Julia Taylor, who was a loveable fun loving girl. She made me laugh. Anything that could make me laugh was a fantastic distraction and relief from the grief that I was hiding inside. Of course, finding the funny side to everything usually meant mild delinquency and infuriating the teachers because that was definitely amusing at the time. Well, it was funny to us, but obviously not to them. Perhaps that was actually one way where I showed my own form of cruelty, which I was to realise later.

Julia soon introduced me to smoking, a habit which I took up at the age of nine—and it made me feel lighter, at least temporarily. I felt like I belonged to the "smoking gang" and that I was grown up. We sat at the back of the buses and smoked together, continuing to find laughter in anything we could. Not surprisingly, this time in my life triggered an addiction that took me a long time to conquer. The addiction was far safer than experiencing the pain of grief. Smoking into the lungs and polluting the breath is as much of a death wish as one could have. It didn't help when Dad caught me smoking and then he would threaten to punish me for it. Inside I laughed, because the truth was that I was already in punishment over my unresolved emotions.

My smoking led to me lying to my parents. Back in those days, my school lunch money was enough to buy a packet of 10 Number 6, so I also starved myself to buy the cigarettes. Food or cigarettes? It was an easy choice at the time. I am so grateful to have experienced the pain, the grief, and the addiction. Whether addicts are addicted to drugs or alcohol, I know the pain they are disguising. Instead of attracting hatred and scorn, they need love and lots of it to help them recover and transform their life to something that they are and feel truly inspired by—in a very real and genuine way. And love is what The Demartini Method® can bring to the hearts of many.

Science now believes or supposes that there is a gene which actually causes people to be become addicted to certain things—in other words, an addictive personality, if you will. My recent attendance of The Prophecy Experience™ with Dr J F Demartini shed further light on evolution and genetics. As we evolve, human emotions can send messages to the DNA and switch certain genetic traits on or off. It is now believed that whilst we inherit the genes of each parent, at the time of conception, aspects can be switched on or off. Therefore, if we switch on addiction and addiction is about covering up feelings, then certainly the death of a loved one would be one way the Universe might wake you up to that fact that you were burying your feelings in the first place.

My smoking addiction saw me smoke a packet of twenty a day for the next 15 years with several abortive attempts at giving up. I then kicked the habit for many years only to begin the sorry addiction again which followed me from the UK to Australia, and saw me change from smoking tobacco to chewing gum. I finally needed a drug to get me off the gum, which I had chewed for two long years. I laughed when I said to the Doctor, "What if I get addicted to the drug?" She laughed too.

Don't be fooled, just because the smoking has stopped, it does not mean that it is the end of everything associated with it. It now means that what was being suppressed has to come to the surface—all of the emotions. Only this time, I continue to work through it using The Demartini Method®. I am inspired to share my experience and process with others so that they too can benefit from using this science to make radical changes in their lives. Remember, it's my mission to understand this work as an opportunity to change, and then share it with others who are struggling too. I hope to bring light to their plight, so to speak.

Messing about foolishly with Julia began to get me into trouble. I was caught skipping school. The story goes like this: the class were meeting at the swimming baths before school, and one friend called Heather had decided to skip the swim. I did the swim and was asking other school girls where my friend Julia was. They told me that she was hiding outside so I went and found her. She was with Heather and they both asked me to join them in skipping school. "Yeah," was my thought. Go with my buddies who I have great laughs with or go to school and face the bullies? Well yes, it was an easy decision to make. So we frolicked along the banks of the River Severn on a beautiful English summer's day. We were doing handstands and cartwheels, laughing at funny stories and generally being cheerful, sharing jokes and doing whatever we could to make each other laugh. In some sweet way, we were drawn to each other for the purposes of finding relief from grief…they definitely had their own fair share in their own lives.

Our laughter didn't last very long. We became conscious of a man on the other side of the river who appeared to be following us. I won't go into all of the details of what happened, but I will say that it shocked us beyond what our minds could comprehend at the time as young women. I felt really scared now and my mind was thinking a thousand thoughts all at once: which way to run, how to avoid being caught. After all, we were supposed to be in school. I was 13 years old. So I did what I always do when I'm in a pickle—I cried. At least I was with my friends. Eventually, after running for a long time, we got back to the town where we soon felt safer. I remember wanting to be with my parents and I completely regretted the idea of having skipped school, however I was obliged to remain silent and not tell a soul. We were obviously caught out for not being at school. It seems so obvious to me now that the teachers would notice our absence but I didn't think that at thirteen. I was so naive and immersed in my own world.

That weekend I had gone camping with the Girl Guides which was a great distraction from the ugly events of the previous Friday. When I returned, just seeing the look on my Dad's face as he came down the driveway, I knew, with that magic intuition of mine that something bad was happening. The haunting memories and the sick pit in my stomach all came flooding back. Oh boy, I was in big trouble. The questioning and interrogation over why I had skipped school, what had made me do it; I clammed up. I had nothing to say, and no reason to give. I knew that if I said I did it because I thought it would be fun and it meant I did not have to face the school bullies would not have been acceptable, it was easier to have them believe whatever they wanted. The truth was not enough. After that, I was 'banned' from going around with Julia. it broke my heart to see the look on her face when I told her that I wouldn't be playing with her any more. It was a hard thing to do, yet at the same time it was a blessing too, as Julia might have got me into deeper trouble than I needed to be in.

I recall that not long after that, Heather and another girl from class both ran away to Birmingham. Now that would have got me into deep trouble. Julia said she wasn't bothered, and that my parents were snobs, but I knew it had hurt her. Soon after that I befriended Valerie. Valerie was also a fun loving and risk taking child. In fact there were four of us who were friends—Susan, Anna, Valerie and I. We used to play tennis non-stop all summer. Every break time we had, we lived and breathed Wimbledon, pretending to be Jimmy Connors serving, or Billy Jean King doing a great shot. This time I could immerse myself in sport and movement and I was doing it with three friends who made it great fun and there was always lots of laughter. If Julia was a loveable and fun-loving Valerie's risk taking would take things to a whole new level. Again, it was a great distraction from the pain. With Valerie I would have "adventures" like you could only dream about: great fun, great laughs, and the great outdoors. Valerie would cry with me over my sisters and tell me that she knew how I felt. I loved her for that, as it felt like I had a sister that I could share things with. Growing up together we would stand naked and compare our bits.

Valerie was envious of me, I had bigger boobs. Valerie was always getting into some kind of trouble, and it seemed so exciting to me.

At the age of 14 she was left alone by her parents one day. She decided that she wanted to try out her sisters Harley Davidson motorbike. So she rode to our friend Susanne's where the bike then broke down and they had to push it home—and I mean she had to push it for ten kilometres. Meanwhile her mother had arrived back to find the garage doors open, lights on, no Valerie and no bike. I recall her telling me that she got a big hiding for it, but we did laugh at the shock her mother would have had. She was a real "St. Trinian" as I call her—the name was derived from the Ronald Searle, fictional English girl's boarding school; a comedy where the school girls got up to no good. The relationship did eventually break down because I was not such a big risk taker.

As you can see, people around me tried to offer an outlet for the repressed emotions of loss and grief, but surprisingly I kept a tight lid on it and that would have taken a great deal of emotional strength, somehow my mind and body had to find a way of relieving the grief. I am so grateful for the fun and laughter; it took me to a world of freedom that allowed me to escape the hard harsh grey landscape that grief entails.

Focusing on sporting activities allowed me to focus my mind, a kind of meditation. I would practice my sports, gymnastics and tennis and concentrate on the small improvements that could be made to my game or my routines. This focus and attention to detail absorbed my mind from needing to think about other things. The benefits to me physically, mentally and health wise are still apparent today and I am full of gratitude to have been given that opportunity in my life.

CHAPTER 4

Teenage Growing Pains

"The turning point in the process of growing up is when you discover the core of strength within you that survives all hurt."

Max Lerner, The Unfinished Country, 1950

As I grew into my teenage years, I had an ache in my heart—I was hungry for love. It was a fantasy that a relationship with a male would provide me with my identity and somehow help me to feel whole again. I believed the right relationship would repair the grief. How wrong could I be? Let me tell you about my first love. It was on a school holiday. Never had I seen such a gorgeous looking man as he passed my seat on the school bus. We were going on a ski trip to Austria and there was me thinking that I did not stand a chance as I surveyed the other beautiful looking girls, I wondered who he would pick. I didn't put myself in the gorgeously attractive bracket. However it was me that Paul sat next to at the airport. I was chuffed to bits, but tried to conceal my delight. Once we were at the resort, we snuck away for time together at night, sitting on the balcony watching the stars. During the day I got my skis carried for me, which at 14 was one hell of a catch. I loved Paul. Then one day he finished with me, saying that his mother thought we were both too serious and too young to be in the relationship. My heart broke. I cried for two weeks at least, every night writhing in pain. I even remember feeling, "This is like losing my sisters all over again."

Perhaps the message is this: when you can deal with your feelings with an open heart, recurring events like this will stop being put in front of you. Loss and more loss, the heart feels it, the body absorbs it. However, in the truth of love, there is never a loss without a gain. Once we are guided by The Demartini Method®, our perceptions of loss can change and we can see the beauty of the gain. Enlightenment is definitely the key to experiencing the turnaround, as you will discover later in this book.

After Paul and I moved on in our own lives, I dated another boy. He was charming, educated and pretty suave. Shrewsbury school was where the famous Darwin was educated and it would seem that Greg was to take me through life's evolutionary process. Only this time around, the Universe wanted to give me an even stronger wake up call to find a powerful way to deal with loss.

After a considerable period of dating, the relationship fizzled out for Greg. He went to University and, not surprisingly, his values were changing. This might sound humorous, but a repetitive broken heart syndrome could easily be a classified as a disease—I know with certainty I'm far from being the only person who has experienced this. I recall being so distraught when he told me it was over between us, that I was prepared, at 16 years old, to beg on my knees for him to stay with me. I could not comprehend that I was with these boyfriends and it was not working out for me…or them. It certainly did not make sense to me nor was it in line with the social, family or church rules that all girls should be married as a virgin. Rules that I blindly bought into and which were not really helping me at all. I figured that I must have been such an awful person to receive what felt like all this suffering. I also recall the horrified look on his face because I was prepared to beg for the relationship to continue. What a sign of weakness and low self-esteem! Yet, it's true, and there's absolutely nothing to hide here, my esteem was at rock bottom.

How cruel life can appear to be sometimes. It's like a tsunami when it destroys all the silly fragile fantasies that people have about life and how life should be. It delivers a sharp slap and an often harsh reality in its place. So often when people experience events like I did, they perceive that they've been dumped, that they are unwanted or rejected—and all of the feelings of nothingness. That was exactly it for me; I felt like a nothing. But, what a great gift! In that moment, when I am and feel that I am nothing, I discover that I am everything. As I am destroyed, I will then create and build in its place.

Powerfully all is not in your awareness at the time, and it has taken me many lessons to come to an understanding of this. So what do I mean by it? Well in order to be able to write this book and to have a strong and consistent message that has the ability to create a powerful shift in you that will lead you to the truth of life I, Lynn, have chosen a path in a kind of blind faith that sees me experience some of life's hardest challenges. I can only cope with whatever it is at the time. If I knew what the future was going to bring to me, back then, I may just have stopped at that point but what you will discover in the next chapters will help you understand what I mean when I say, "Powerfully all is not in your awareness at the time." At the final point where I felt that my endurance was failing, I was offered the key to unlock the true potential of my life journey, and I am forever grateful and humbly thankful to God for allowing me to live this experience and journey and to share it with you, for your discovery too.

And so, as evolution continued on its way, my next life lesson came with the discovery that I was pregnant at the age of 17 years old. How did that happen, you wonder? Well, although Greg ended our relationship he used to flit in and out, taking me for lunch or for a walk and on one completely unplanned occasion we loved each other. I found out that I was pregnant just as I started at the Buckinghamshire College of Higher Education at Chalfont St. Giles. My parents dropped me off and within a week or two I took a pregnancy test and discovered what 'the line' meant. Oh! How my head spun. I knew no-one around me, I was in a strange environment and I had no-one to talk to. I knew that my parents would disown me—that was a certainty. I called Greg and told him. I knew somewhere inside of me that I had a vague hope he would be happy with the news that we had a potential child together—and that he would also want to marry me.

Uh oh, fantasy land! Greg was shocked and the first thing he asked me was, "How do I know it's mine?" What a kick in the guts that was. It felt like another sledgehammer, what was he saying to me? Was he implying that I was a 'tart'? That I had slept around with other men while I was with him? I felt that he'd been heartless and uncaring in his comments—with a total lack of empathy. I now appreciate with some humour that because of our relationship ending, I am no longer stuck in the middle of the Shropshire countryside, rearing a family and feeling bored with life—and my relationship. Instead, I am now here in Australia embarking on my journey home, and it's an inspiring journey that fills me with love and a gratitude for all the things that have happened in my life.

As it was designed to happen for my life at the time, I lost the child and struggled greatly, experiencing my own nightmares and pain. What was unloved kept repeating for me. Sometimes at night I failed to stifle my agony and I would let out wounded cries in my sleep. I wanted to gag myself for fear that someone would hear me. My next door neighbour, who was a Christian and religious—whatever that means—would look straight through me with her eyes. The same intuition that informed me ahead of time about my sisters passing told me that she was caring and supporting me, even though I felt or perhaps wanted to believe that no-one was. I think her name was Clare. Thank you Clare for being part of the perfection in the Universe, making sure that nothing is ever truly missing.

My loss is my biggest lie to everyone around and to myself. I chose to keep silent about what had happened. I believed that the main reason for my decision was a fear that I would be disowned and fear of the pain that it would bring. This fear of rejection was based on historic family and religious values but also having experienced abandonment by the twins. There was also a protective side to not wanting my parents to go through more anguish. Yet the more I learned the less I appeared to know. I now fully understand that it was simply meant to be for the carving of my soul and for me to be able to help many others who go through similar situations. It is a choice I made to experience these events and to know the anguish of them. Sounds crazy hey?

It is astounding that I found the inner strength to bottle the emotions of such deeply ingrained loss. The scars were deep and had been gouged deeper. Many people would crack under such pressure, but I didn't. I carried on my daily routines as if nothing had happened, yet inside my heart was heavily burdened. I recall crying more when my dog passed away than at my sister's funeral. At times of course, it would get too much and I would cry myself to sleep but this was many years after the events. I believe that Mum,

Dad, Lauren and I are all on a remarkable journey that will free us and our family for generations to come! The journey is unfolding continually and is a process that I am following and trusting in my conversations with God that I am on a path of truth and light.

College was a weird place for me. I found it difficult to relate to the other students. I could not share my innermost thoughts and feelings and so building authentic relationships was difficult to do. I had friends that I hung around with but they were distracting themselves from their own hidden challenges and so most of the time we were all taking life far less seriously than we should. It was exciting at first, okay the next, and then I wanted to get away when it came to the final year. I felt there were too many big egos trying to impress people with their achievements or their plans and dreams for the future, and too many fools. I laugh because I am not sure which one I was; a big ego or a big fool. Throughout college my friends had no idea of the real pain I was experiencing, and I never talked about it because I figured it was so intense, so heavy and so deep that they really would not want to know. They were young students on campus who were having fun, and that was the 'right' thing to do. I was simply a young student on a very different path. The thing that impresses me most through all of this—through every corner, twist and turn of my experiences—is that I now have the ability to see it all exactly for what it was, awareness of soul.

It's incredible to me that I could even have experienced so much intense emotion; enough that it could have stopped me in my tracks—but that wasn't to be. There was so much more to come. You are probably wondering what worse things could happen after so much had already taken place and when I reflect on it, I'm bemused because I know it's quite shocking. I laugh because I know the story is mine, and I chose to live it. I know how much I have gone through up until this day in order to be able to guide you in healing your own grief—whatever the area of life it might be that you are experiencing bereavement in. It makes me realise how sensitive yet strong we are as human beings. We feel everything but can still withstand so much.

As you read the next chapter, you will see how I was now firmly ingrained in a repetitive cycle that was to culminate in a long series of chaotic dynamics in my marriages. God's gift for me continued in intimate relationships until I reached a breakdown point, the one that led me, along with my career, to the discovery of a brand new perspective on life. The chapter will build a picture of how our relationships are designed to reflect what we have not owned and loved in ourselves. We have already seen a little of this with my earlier boyfriends—in how they were trying to wake me up to the perfection of my past and to heal my grief—and this next chapter shares what happened as I progressed on, living out the themes of loss and denying parts of myself.

CHAPTER 5

Marriages Made In Heaven

*"Marriage is not designed for happiness; it's designed
to wake up in you the parts you have not owned."*
Dr. John Demartini

As I finished my college education, I continued living in Buckinghamshire,
a UK county of great wealth and prosperity. My first job was working just
outside the City of London in a place called Hounslow for an IT computer
hardware company called Data General. I lived with four other students
in a four bedroom house. Our lives were fun, chaotic and crazy. We were
forever looking for fun things to do that would make us all laugh. We
would sit together for hours talking, laughing, and watching movies. We
would have fun dubbing over the top of recorded programs, each choosing
a character from programs like Dallas.

We would go out at night up to the Mansion where they recorded
the very scary *Tales of the Unexpected*. We would draw lots as to who was
to get out of the car in the dark of the night and creep right up to the front
door of the derelict mansion. It scared us no end. We would take trips out
in Tim's open top sports car, go down the to the river bank and then sit
in the summer sun and drink beer all afternoon. Back at home we would
have timed races on who could actually put the ironing board up—not that

as students we ever bothered ironing, so it was funny to see how the boys struggled to get the ironing board to stand up.

During this time, I shared the house with a fellow student and my boyfriend Steve. Steve was a lovely guy. He was of one of two brothers. Steve was a funny guy who was gentle and sensitive. He had also lost his mother early in his life. We spent many hours together as friends before we ever sussed that we might 'like' each other. There was a lot of talking to my girlfriends and asking the question, "Well, do you think he likes me?" and prompting them to tell me what I wanted to hear and not what I was thinking "I think he sees me as just a friend". I recall Steve telling me that it was the same from his perspective: he was unsure whether I saw him just as a friend, or whether I liked him and wanted him to be my boyfriend.

Steve and I eventually got together and it was fulfilling. We had great fun, we explored, we talked, we shared, and we loved. There was always a sense of adventure and fun; we lived in the moment for the moment. We spent time with our friends down by the river banks of the Thames, enjoying delightful picnics and laughter, or spending time in the peaceful town of Windsor, or visiting the zoo and laughing at the monkeys. I recall going to Wimbledon and laughing at the fact that we queued for hours in the sun and then when we finally made it to the courts, rain stopped play. At least it was an experience we shared together. Eventually over time, my feelings for him fizzled out and dissolved into a "brotherly love" kind of feeling. Have you ever experienced that with a partner where the chemistry you experienced at the beginning started to wear off into normalcy? After a while, I had no desire to kiss him. I even became pleased and grateful for him to be with someone else and experience other women. I would tell him that I wouldn't mind if he did go and have sex with other women, as I knew I wasn't providing what he needed. It was a fact which I know must have hurt him, but at least I was honest with him and it gave him the opportunity to find the love he deserved.

The feelings drove me to despair and discomfort. It was very confusing for me and led me back to thinking about my childhood sweetheart, Paul, who I had broken up with right after he had proposed to me. Perhaps the feelings I had with Steve were actually a trigger for my unconscious desire to go back to Paul and resolve my earlier issues. Although I am not certain of this, what I do know is that I was thinking of Paul a lot and wanted to see him again. I felt that I had to get away from Steve to explore my life in greater colour and detail. I didn't know what it meant but I felt strongly drawn to be close to Paul again, who lived in Shrewsbury.

You are probably wondering why I dumped Paul for proposing to me. The fact that he wanted to marry me when I was so young all added to the confusion of my emotions, I was terrified. Perhaps it was a fear of commitment; or maybe unresolved fears relating to the death of my sisters. Or, perhaps my soul knew I had other destined work to undertake. His proposal saw me run a mile and, although I knocked him down hard, he said he would 'wait forever' for me to change my mind. Of course, as soon as I did, he was no longer interested! Destiny works in this way. We become hungry for something and destiny makes sure we don't get it!

I returned to Shrewsbury, originally my home town, and lived there for a few years. I met up with Paul again while I was there only to be knocked back by him returning to a girl he had lived with for several years whilst I was away at college. Young love is so confusing and it can hurt if you don't see things from a bigger perspective. Being rejected by Paul after my rejecting him years earlier was a reminder for me to really understand who people are, what they value and what's important to them—and not to take people for granted. We all have the desire inside of us to be loved and appreciated by the people in our lives—and Paul was no different.

The day I was rejected is etched on my mind. I walked through the parklands called the "Quarry" in the middle of Shrewsbury Town, fighting back my tears of unrequited love. I recall sitting in a chair at the bandstand which had been set up for a performance. I sat and listened to the silent music, and shed silent tears. A voice inside me whispered, "Lynn, pick yourself up and do not cry any more". So that's what I decided to do. I stopped crying and put on a brave face, the one I was used to putting on. I gave up on Shrewsbury and moved to Lancashire. On reflection, if I had married Paul, my life would not be what it is today and so I am grateful for turning him down, and also for him turning me down. Even after my move from Shropshire, Paul and I maintained contact, although it was on rare occasions. While I dated different guys over the next few years, I couldn't seem to re-establish the same level of love and trust and so all relationships appeared both boring and pointless to me.

When I returned to Lancashire it turned out to be a great party venue. Blackpool is the Mecca of the country. It's Las Vegas, Paris, and the Gold

Coast all in one. It's attractive, sensational and alluring for both young and old. It's the only place I have come across where you tend not to feel out of place regardless of your age. All ages mix together in the clubs. Dancing is something that I love—it makes me feel alive. I have often felt that I experience a peak if I'm dancing to great music. I think my dance fever was born through John Travolta, and I thank him for that. Abba also undoubtedly had an influence in that way.

As a young girl who was slim and attractive, I would party like it was 1999! I loved dancing, and I felt dancing was me. I see the amazing and wonderful dancers they have today, but back then it was tamer and less dramatic. I felt at a loving peace when dancing and I rarely shied away from moving and grooving. There is something about dancing which can bring flow and vitality back to you no matter what is occurring in your life—you can immerse yourself in the music and in the movement. All your worries and concerns can dissolve into thin air, and it is as though you become centred and balanced in that moment, completely present with the music.

I was confident when dancing. I danced in nightclubs from the time I was thirteen years old (beginning in Shrewsbury Town in a club called Tiffany's) and have danced throughout my life, even up to only a year ago. I love the music, I love the rhythm and melody, and I love the beat. Now at home, when I get the opportunity to turn the music up and dance, I do, and then I often feel content and inspired. Music and dance are a key source of rejuvenation and love for me. I do believe that I have passed on this bug to my daughter Lauren, as she is now familiar with her mother's Saturday Night Fever.

Nightclubs are great places. I can hear Mum now saying, "Yes, but they will get you into drugs". It made me ask, where was she when I was surfing clubs from the age of thirteen? I never once took drugs in a nightclub! I was never even offered drugs in a nightclub. I was remotely aware that certain types of people took drugs, but it just seemed like a really dangerous thing to me: like risking a life. I sometimes felt that my mother had the worst view of me, why on earth would I do such a thing? I realise now that her fears of losing another child after her two daughters slipped away were making her over protective.

As girls, we always hoped we would meet our "true love" in the club. I am now almost convinced that you never meet anyone in a nightclub worth marrying or being with on a long term basis—it's not to say it's impossible, but I met many guys there then spent most of the time avoiding them as they were lecherous and rude. I used to find it insulting when a geek would try it on. Little did I realise that I was that geek!

For a while I worked in a pub serving drinks. After the pub closed, I would go dancing at a nightclub, in a never-ending but hopeful search for my partner. It never happened and I became distraught that after the mess-up with my childhood sweetheart, nothing would ever be right, ever again! And nothing was ever right apart from my thoughts and the pattern I was following. Soon the pattern was broken by the appearance of an old friend.

My old school friend Valerie came to live in Manchester around 1987. I would spend many hours at her place, recapturing our youth. It was through her that I met Miles—he was a fun, lovely and caring, sensitive soul. That was on the one hand. I believed that Miles came into my life at that exact point where I was on the rebound from another rejection. Oh, how the Universe loves to teach lessons! They say that love is blind. I had just bought a property near Preston and before long Miles was spending all his time with me, and very soon he asked me to marry him. I was twenty six years old at the time. Wow, I felt that I was loved at last! I laugh when I look back, as it almost seems pathetic and naive to me now but that was it. Mum began preparing for the "wedding of the year" and who can blame her, her only daughter was getting married! For whatever reason, I felt unable to question her decisions over my wedding and how the big day was going to unfold. I lay down and accepted whatever she said. I could not say what I did or did not want for the wedding. I felt it would only upset Mum and, I was not going to upset her, she had been upset enough over my sisters dying. You see, I was so imbalanced in my thoughts, so uncomfortable and so completely disempowered that I felt I had no choice but to keep quiet and do what Mum said. Ask yourself, how fair was that to my mother, really? I blamed her for years about the perceived control she had over me, when in reality it was me controlling the situation. The truth for me was that if I wasn't certain what I wanted for a wedding day, then perhaps I was also not certain on what I wanted in a marriage.

As events progressed and a few arguments with Miles occurred, I recall visiting Mum and Dad and crying to them. Mum said, "Well, what do you want to do?" I felt I could not upset Mum and all her preparations. What if I called it off? I could not face the truth. I was scared that it was the wrong decision, I was scared that I would make Mum angry, scared that I had wasted lots of money and that it was way too close to the actual wedding day to change my mind. At the time I wasn't aware of how to balance my perceptions and so I also missed the chance to see what a waste it might be—of my own time as well as Miles's—to get married when my heart and inspiration weren't there. Fortunately or unfortunately, it is sometimes easier to deny it than it is to face the truth.

I was trying to fill a void in my own life. The void I was trying to fill was one in which I desperately wanted to be loved for me. I still had the fantasy that a partner was going to make my inner emotional traumas more bearable. I was such a people pleaser that I believed if I kept them happy and did what they wanted me to do, they would love me. Of course, this was the fastest way to get rejected and build an even bigger fear of rejection in the future. When we are in denial about the truth of love, we distance ourselves from God, yet in doing so we learn more about God. Ego can often get in the way. Ego separates you from the awareness of divine intelligence in the world, and it teaches us all about yin and yang, good and evil, positive and negative—the two sides of every coin in life. My lessons were coming hard and fast. I backed away from what might have been the truth. I went ahead and had one of the most wonderful days of my life in my mind. Nothing that Miles did after our wedding day could take away the beautiful and blissful day that I'd had. The joyful wedding was shortlived. The morning after was disgraceful. I recall Miles asking me to pay the hotel bill in front of the reception. I wanted the floor to swallow me up, I wanted to cry, I felt worthless, and I felt publicly humiliated. It was so embarrassing. I was 26 years old at the time. I was not a youngster, but certainly immature for my age. Even in my youth however, my intuition was accurate and the fears that I had chosen to suppress were soon founded. My marriage with Miles lasted six weeks…Yes, six weeks! The finer, more graphic details of the marriage and its breakdown are recounted in another book in the *Authentic Results* book series; however I will say that in my perception the six weeks of this marriage was hell for me. The moment that fantasy wedding day was over, my perception of hell began.

I simply had to extract myself from him—otherwise I think one of us may very well have ended up in the morgue. The subsequent divorce was long, traumatic and it took more than two years to resolve. It also cost a considerable amount of time, money and emotion—not just for me but for my parents as well. My desire to protect them frequently seemed to end up causing them more anguish. I moved some 500 kilometres away from

Miles in a bid to get away from the memories and start a new life. I quickly learned that there was to be no escaping the reality of my own emotions about this 'hell'. One day while I was at work in High Wycombe, I looked out of the window only to see Miles walking down the road with my godson. Of all the places I could have seen him; this was more than a coincidence. I had absolutely no doubt left in my mind that day that God truly does work in mysterious ways—the very person I was trying to escape from was right there in front of me! Not understanding the perfection yet, or even that there was one; I thought it was cruel fate.

I chose to hide and look over my shoulder for months afterwards; forever suspicious that Miles would find me and I would then enter into a living hell again. It's actually pretty amazing how the Universe can make these things happen. Or rather, as a correction, it is me working with the Universe to make these things happen. It made me ask even bigger questions about life, like: Are we really the creators of our own realities?

It was in High Wycombe, Buckinghamshire, that I met Guy. I was first attracted to his voice. It was strong and deep with a hint of a chuckle and cheekiness. We used to spend a lot of time talking on the telephone as he was providing support on a project that I had worked on. The project was intense and for six months I was living in a small hotel West of Wycombe. I started dating Guy and after about six months he proposed to me. I said yes with very little hesitancy, if at all. I didn't stop to think that the project was ending and I was supposed to be returning to Lancashire, and maybe it was all too easy for Guy to pull my strings. No, I was infatuated with him. I hadn't had a feeling like this for years.

We decided to build a house together with the view that we would marry and move in together. It all went well. I recall a couple of bad arguments, and my denial kicked in yet again, but this was not enough to tell me not to do it. And as sure as we had planned it, Guy and I were married and moved into our lovely home. At last it seemed that my life was going to pull back together into the fairy-tale idealism that I kept buying into. You know the one: "We will all live happily ever after," and at last I can be a "respectable wife." I was certain this marriage would take away the pain of the previous problems, that it would restore my health and sanity, and along with it, my belief and trust and marriage. My fantasy was just getting bigger but little did I know it was about to fall apart right in front of my eyes.

The marriage lasted approximately nine months as our communication was rapidly deteriorating. Eventually I said that I would take a break and visit my parents. Guy agreed, and I set off on the long trip up to the North of England, crying most of the way. I never returned to that relationship, except to pick up my belongings which happened to be most of the house contents. I was undoubtedly devastated to find my second marriage also in tatters. Not for the first time in my life, I experienced a deep sense of loss and grief. This time it wasn't over the physical passing of a loved one—it was the loss of a relationship, and actually, the loss of a fantasy that I had been holding onto so tightly. I struggled with the idea of facing up to reality.

How was I going to face up to everyone? I felt sure that I would be ridiculed. My ego was screaming and I failed to calm it down. I felt so low and depressed that I even considered taking my own life. In an effort to salvage any morsel of self-worth I might have left, I decided to stay in Lancashire and live at home with my parents. That was an adjustment in itself. I can honestly say that I am appreciative of my parents; I am fortunate and know that many can't return home to the fold and start afresh—especially at the age of 29.

Don't get me wrong, it was not easy for them or for me. They were reeling in agony at my two failed marriages almost as much as I was—except they rarely said anything about it in an effort to help me save myself. I was feeling very much like a failure. My pain also included my parents' pain. The very thing I wanted to avoid was happening, and I was making them face their pain all over again. I literally thank God today that I now understand there was a balance in this situation, and that my parents were just as intent as I to be together during the times of transition that I experienced. At the time, I felt that I could control things and as a result of that, I felt totally responsible for everything that had happened. I believe this might even have stretched back as far as the passing of my twin sisters. I not only struggled with my own emotional baggage but I perceived that I suffered my parents' emotional baggage too.

The underlying and now increasingly apparent themes of my life unfolded through another area: they'd reached from my childhood years through to my relationships in the younger adult years of my life. First it was my sisters' deaths, then my first boyfriend, and now through two divorces and relationships that didn't work. I was overwhelmed. I was fast approaching a point in my life where I was burning out from the unresolved emotional charges of my years. Depression set in. To this day, I haven't truly labelled that time in my life as having 'depression' for many reasons. Goodness, if you have 'depression' on your work records, almost any employer will have hesitancy over bringing you onto their team. It will "go against you." And so I experienced what I will refer to (for the sake of logic) as depression. Writing this now, I know that I actually didn't or couldn't even identify it as that at the time—because my mind was in such a scramble. All in all, that time in my life taught me how to be resilient and a true fighter; above and beyond anything I had experienced before. I often think of the song 'Eye of the Tiger' and fighting for survival when I reflect back on my 'depression'.

Of course, the true fight really comes after a rejection, after feeling unloved, after feeling that life is too hard to live. It came in the form of Dad getting angry at me because I wanted to go for a drink with a friend, a non-white work friend. Dad blew a gasket! What was I doing? How could I shame him, in front of his golf friends, in the small town of Lytham St. Annes by going for a drink with a 'black man'? Me, who had been divorced twice!

I felt worthless; somehow my loving parents had a knack of revealing my addiction to their support or fear of rejection and abandonment. Only this time it reduced me to less than nothing. I sat with my nothingness for an hour at "Granny Bay" contemplating suicide. The lake is beautiful and inviting. All I needed to do was drive the car into the lake. It was not to be. Eventually, as I sat there in my depressed state, I suddenly heard the car radio, repeatedly singing "Jesus loves me". I heard it and I heard it again, over and over for what seemed like an eternity and finally it dawned on me that I had a reason for living and it was because Jesus loves me.

That was a big turning point. I am always amazed at that old song that came on the radio, it saved my life! Or rather I chose life. Of course I did, I have a mission to get on with and fulfil and I know I am here to support others who may have imbalanced perceptions and be suffering unnecessarily. I was very much put off by marriage and boyfriends. I worked and pursued my career. I left Lancashire and moved to Essex. I had completed a Master's Degree in Information Technology and Ford could provide me with immeasurable experience in IT systems. I worked for Ford for a couple of years and then an agency offered me a role I could not refuse—working for a software ERP company as a consultant.

The role was brilliant; I got to travel abroad and see a lot of Holland and I also got to travel to Venezuela. It was a very difficult period for the organisation and there was a general fear that the company would go bust, leaving the salaries unpaid. I therefore decided to jump ship and went to work for a new setup, trying to win eCommerce contracts to build websites. I believed this would give me up-to-date skills and would be an adventure. It certainly turned out to be true. This was where I met my Stuart. We worked together in the same job role for about eight months before we started dating. This made me believe I knew him fairly well. Of course I completely blinkered my view and only saw the parts that I wanted to see. Despite many troubled arguments and some of the strangest behaviour I accepted his proposal of marriage in the belief that we both wanted similar things, a life built around trust, children, security, sport, adventure and good careers. Without going into details at this stage, it was one of the most difficult relationships I could have ever entered into, and probably because of the past, I was able to be more accommodating of some of the adverse behaviour from Stuart. Was this a good thing?

We planned a marriage; can you believe a church wedding? I was still somehow fixated with the belief that I had never done a wrong thing in my previous two marriages, and that it would be okay with God if I remarried in a church. Now, if that isn't a big fantasy I don't know what is. Stuart managed to halt the church wedding. You'll have to read the book titled Breaking Through Divorce to fully appreciate what extent he had to go to in order to break my fantasy. Once those arrangements were over, we split up for a while. I stayed away from him; I think we had traumatised ourselves too much.

I went on a skiing holiday with friends from outer London, it was the perfect distraction as I had a lovely group of buddies and we would have great fun skiing the slopes of Italy or France. If anything makes me feel the blood run through my veins it is skiing in the mountains! Danger, fun, physical exhaustion, great food absorption, exhilaration, laughter, tears, wind, cold, love, love of the mountain, love of friends, love of life. The mountain was healing in so many ways. When I returned to England I felt more centred and calm.

I spoke with Stuart and all was calm with him. That was when we moved forward to make the most "volcanic" of relationships come into being. My daughter Lauren was the output of that volcanic energy from the moment of inception to the moment of her birth. The relationship could never be sustained. I didn't always trust what Stuart would say or do and he lived on many different levels. In saying that, he did no more than we all do. He was actually acting as a mirror to show me the parts I had not loved about myself. However, I struggled with the things that in reality I had created, I struggled with being pregnant and learning these things about him. Little realising that he was teaching me about myself. I tried very hard, I tried my best to stay with the one I loved. I could not tolerate the shouting, the comments, the control, the fear, all traits that I now know I needed to own and love! It certainly was one big lesson—one that I am grateful for.

After several months of marriage and following the birth of my daughter, I finally broke down after repeated calls to the police, as I felt fear for my life and fear for my daughter's. I gave our relationship another chance but it did not work. It was like whatever door I opened it would be closed. I never understand the "vindictive" wife syndrome because I did everything I possibly could to ensure that my little girl got to spend time with her Dad. That was even too difficult one of us needed absolute control, and by the time I discovered that, I also found that my identity had been stolen.

Yes, I had a one hundred page credit file, full of applications and unpaid bills. It took me two weeks to recover from the shock; in my perception I believed he had done it and at the same time I could not believe that my husband could do such a thing. He denied it too. I then had to pluck up the courage to go to the police to investigate my suspicions; in my heart I did not want my daughter's father to be the one who had done this. It was then that I knew it was time to take hold of the reins and look after my own health, as well as for my daughter. For me, the message was clear I needed time alone to contemplate and understand what was happening in my life. Eventually I decided to take a course called Pattern Changing, to understand more about myself.

So there you go! That depicts the highly successful marriages of Lynn Hope Thomas: a mess and a melee of mixed and muddled emotions.

Repeated knocks and cruelty, repeated messages from the Universe but no real pick up from me. It just seemed to be a never-ending mass of pain, drain, and no gain. As we get to *Chapter 13—The True Light of Loss* we uncover what was really happening in these marriages. They really were made in heaven as the Chapter title suggests. And as I learn of the truth, I can now say thank you for and have gratitude to each of the lovely souls who gave me that experience.

CHAPTER 6

Career And Marriage Challenges

"The rate of change is not going to slow down any time soon. If anything, competition in most industries will probably speed up even more in the next few decades."

John P. Kotter

The quote above explains to me very clearly why the rate of change in my career over the decades has sped up considerably. It's a very astute point because as Dr J F Demartini explains, if we can see what we perceive as negative events as 'on the way' and not 'in the way', then it becomes fuel for our mission and destiny, instead of holding us back. And I myself have equally, during the past three decades, seen a great number of my changes as 'in the way' and not 'on the way'…until now. For this reason too, they kept repeating themselves. Reading through and hearing about the twists and turns of my working career and life will show you just how strongly loss and grief can impact your business—even if it's not your own—you will see what kind of chaos you can breed when your emotions are unresolved.

I have divided the evolution of my working career into three sections, and I will walk you through the twists and turns of my vocation decade-by-decade. You will see the patterns that developed and the key events that occurred, including the build-up of momentum that ultimately led to my immigration to Australia. If you were to read or hear each of these pieces on its own, you would not see the themes playing out over and over again as clearly as you will by putting my whole story together and seeing the cyclical patterns recurring. They could almost be written out like a musical sonnet—like watching the wonder and beauty of the Universe unfold and realising there are no mistakes. All events are exactly on track in order to deliver my purpose to the Universe. For me it is exhilarating, to finally come to that realisation and allow the breath to run through me. I feel alive and I feel much love.

At school I never knew what I wanted to do when I grew up. I vaguely recall, as a young child at primary school, wanting to either be an astronomer, a comedian or a "go-go" dancer. It is easy to laugh at these seemingly dissimilar careers and wonder how one can find a mix within them. At secondary school, the only real career ambitions appeared to be a choice of becoming a mother, working as a bank clerk (because only men became the bank managers) or become a nurse or even a doctor, if you were bright enough. No one ever truly discussed it with me, no one asked me or made me aware of the possibilities, or how to even begin to determine what you might like to do or be.

Let's be clear here: my parents had great dreams for me, and they certainly wanted me to go to University, but for some reason I was rebellious and did not want to do what they wanted me to do, I wanted to decide for myself. But if only I knew what decision I needed to make, it might have helped. I find it interesting that they often described me as stubborn and strong-minded, and yet inside I felt I had a very limited choice. I *had* to please them: how could I not please them after everything we had gone through? And so, because of this, I tortured myself over and over. I mean, what sort of career was that? Go to University…why would I? Because University meant something! How many children are feeling that today? Why go to University? What are the real job prospects at the end of it? For whatever reason, I could not hear or see the details. I think now, to have made an impression upon me, I needed to have had a job role, named and presented to me, one that excited me and an understanding of the true purpose for acquiring a University degree. It's possible that my inquisitive nature had yet to be unleashed in that part of my brain. I seemed to take at face value that there were "rules" to life and all adults knew what they were, so don't push it. Who the hell was I to question or come up with anything new?

When my parents gave me a broad statement of fact like, "Those who attend University get better money and better jobs", it just did not help to kick in any ambition or yearning. I appreciate and am grateful for learning this point. I hope that I will have more success in teaching my daughter, although it may not be required as she already knew at the age of three what she wanted to do, and so far has not changed her mind! I have since learnt from Dr J F Demartini that it all comes down to values. If they had communicated to me in terms of my values, I would have been able to respond in an appropriate way. Yet, then again I did not know at that point in my heart what I really wanted.

From what I have learnt now about thought, energy and manifestation, it's no wonder my life has been so troubled and traumatic on so many occasions. It's not so much about positive or negative thoughts as many people think. It's about setting out your understanding of your values, and then setting out your mission statement of what you want to be, do and have, not in any kind of order but simultaneously. Most self-help stuff will fill you with positive affirmations and that's fine, it's motivational. However, it is not inspirational. Motivation means you require a force to get you to do what you don't really want to do, whereas inspiration instantly gives you the energy to fulfil your mission. Affirmations that tell you to think positively and be positive, are all nonsense and can actually have a bad influence in your life. It certainly did for me; I felt such a failure for not living up to some of those ideals. Although I am grateful to learn that spending time focusing on the small things about each wonderful day and being grateful is easy to do and it is abundantly rewarding. Believe me, there is plenty of magic out there to be grateful for.

When I finished college I began work in Hounslow, Middlesex. It was just the kind of place where a nice country girl would get depressed— concrete buildings, traffic and smog. Life did not feel that it was working out for me. I lived in a mixed share house that was, at times, rather chaotic. Work was far from where I lived and so I spent a lot of time travelling. Young and clever, my bright ideas were rapidly trodden on. I handed in my notice, telling my boss that I wanted to move to the North of England, back to my home town. If you recall in *Chapter 2—Doctrine of Double Effect* I wanted to return to Shrewsbury to meet up with Paul. My boss was disappointed and tried to talk to me about what was happening in my life but I was so down, I could not talk. He tried again to find out what was going through my mind but I detached myself, and believed that the move back to Shrewsbury would bring me happiness. In making the move, I left my boyfriend behind, and I was very careless about his feelings; however I forgive myself for being so lost at that time.

Back in Shrewsbury I found work at Perkin Engines—manufacturers of Rolls Royce engines. Career-wise I was willingly pursuing my accountancy qualifications. I had finally determined a career by scanning the "Sunday Times" Appointments section and figuring out that Accountancy and Computing paid the top salaries. I had obviously failed to take account of Lawyers and Barristers. If only I knew back then what I know now, why going for just a job means: Just Over Broke. I now know that there is power in dreaming and doing what you love. Gratefully, I did not know it back then otherwise I wouldn't be writing this amazing book and feeling truly inspired and on my mission.

I did have a good time too in Shrewsbury. I worked hard but I also played hard. Playing took the form of nightclubs and dancing plus Shrewsbury has more public houses (or rather "pubs") per head than any other town in England. The British pub is a tradition that will be hard to kill off—a lot fun and good times are had down at the local. In Shrewsbury we would start with a drink in one favourite pub and then walk through the town visiting as many as we could in one evening. The town of Shrewsbury dates back to the Tudor times; there is a wonderful historic look and feel to the town that never dies. All the pubs have low wooden beams and crooked floors. They are painted black and white and have tiny glass windows. I love Shrewsbury Town. You know when I return, usually in the summertime, I can smell the smell of home, the sweet fields, the countryside, the air, the grass, the cows, the farms, the birds, the flowers, the river, the trees, the stones, the castle, the meadows, the Tudor wood, the bus station and all its memories. It is and will always be home.

Anyway, the choice of career was good. Mum and Dad moved to Lancashire to support Dad's business which had opened an office there.

Lancashire anyway was home country to most of our family. We were all Lancashire born and bred. We are strong workers in Lancashire, a county that was renowned for the cotton mills, long before cheaper imports. My grandmother was so fast in the mill that she would be sitting doing her knitting whilst others worked. The Managing Director wanted to fire her when he saw her doing her knitting. He then checked the payroll, and discovered that she was earning the most. He asked, "How come she is paid the most and I always seeing her sitting down? Sack her?" The foreman explained that she was faster than everyone else and so the bonus rates paid to her were handsome. She was then moved to the offices and soon became a monthly paid employee and controlled expenditure.

I worked a few years in Lancashire, living with my parents during this time. I enjoyed the nightlife of Blackpool, which might or could otherwise be known as the "Vegas" of the UK. During the day I worked as an accountant and at night I danced and danced—so very contrasting! I was taking examinations at the time, but studying was minimal as dancing was far more inspiring to me. I see now that I was young and could have followed a dancing career; I could have been that "Go Go" dancer I dreamed of as a little girl. However, I had inherited the family culture of 'work hard, a job's a job, so put your head down and grind'. As a child (and a rebellious one at that) I never challenged what I really needed to challenge, I was so accepting of this hard grind mentality. Still, I had a great time working for a small airline out of Blackpool airport. Our work was cut out for us; the company was three months behind in opening its post! The finances were in a mess. There were essentially two teams: the ticketing girls, and the finance team. How different they were! One of the pretty ticketing girls was dating the boss and was jealous of me. The boss actually liked the comical side to my nature and this enraged his girlfriend beyond belief. The tension in the office could be cut in two with a knife. I recall one girl labelling the office as the "tuffs" and the "toffs"—I will leave you to guess which team fitted which name.

This was all happening around the time that Dallas was the rage on television—looking back now, it was all so comical. I recall working with two chartered accountants who were supporting the backlog in the finances. We had such a great laugh at work, playing tricks on each other and going for nights out in Blackpool. I look back and remember the aggression from Mandy's friends, threatening to "smash my face in" as they wait for me outside work. All I had actually done was set light to Mandy's jealousy by being comical me. Mmm, maybe I did not quite appreciate how I was prickling her fears and how her friends would rally round to support her, then equally the toffs rallied round me and this brought the situation into balance and made for a very interesting work life.

Eventually they decided to move the accounts department to Exeter airport and so I was redundant and I lost the job I adored. I moved to DER TV Rentals, a bit like Radio Rentals here in Australia, they were part of Thorn EMI. There I took a role as a Financial Analyst. I recall the boss noted in his interview papers, "pretty eyes", this is so funny as its deemed unacceptable these days—and yes often as young girls we were subjected to "cheeky" comments, but it was all part of what made work fun in those days! Now it's been taken away from us and we have to be politically correct.

Thorn EMI decided to close the Northwest regional office. Job loss number two. It was at that time when mortgage rates were shooting through the roof at 16%. I had a new mortgage, my second home, I was 20 something and I recall scraping the pennies together to buy milk. The staff in the office were angry about being made redundant. They helped themselves to furniture, carpets filing cabinets, you name it and it disappeared. They even erased the data off the hard disks on their computers. You will also recall in *Chapter 3* it was whilst I was at Thorn EMI that I met Miles through my friend Valerie. I was fortunate to be asked to stay an extra month to assist in the closure, but then after that I was redundant. I always recall how the redundancy affected the older people more than the young ones.

The loss of my job didn't worry me: I was young and I had "pulling power". I got my next job at a wholesale grocer, part of Northern Foods. The pressure to get on board and allow the boss to go on holiday was too much though. I was fed up with being the last person to leave and having to lock up. I guess I was well trusted by them, but this did not seem to make up for the excessive control and demands of the boss. One day, just before he was due to go on holiday, I set off in the car on the motorway heading for work, but the car came off the slipway and returned back home. I just decided that "No!" I did not like the new job and I wasn't going to do it. Youth has so much power. It's unrestrained by the conventions and critique of society. Thank goodness that's the way it is!

I easily managed to get a great job working for a GEC company near British Aerospace. The accountant was called John. I look back and think that the Universe gave me that job simply to see me over the difficulties I would encounter when divorcing Miles. The reason I say this is that John was a kind manager and he gave me lots of freedom. My first divorce was part of my growing up and experiencing stress. My next book in the series will look at divorce in greater depth; it's a whole experience in itself, especially when the divorce is full of bitterness and difficulty. The impact of the divorce, led to Miles telephoning me at work. This became almost intolerable: it was hard to focus on my career and I desperately wanted to conceal what I felt was an embarrassing situation. How was I going to do that?

The next chapter reveals how 'escapism' works in the Universe. You can run but you can't hide away from the truth. No matter how intolerable your situation, learning to face it and feel it, is part of growth, running away simply stores it up for later consumption, and in the meantime you may be wasting years of your life. My purpose is to teach you how to face the challenges, so you can more quickly continue on your way, balanced and allowing you to control your own life, instead of it controlling you. You'll see the tricks that the Universe pulls in order to shock you into awareness. Even today, I still find it just amazing—an ever-unfolding mystery to be solved

CHAPTER 7

Career Development

*"Character cannot be developed in ease and quiet.
Only through experiences of trial and suffering can
the soul be strengthened, vision cleared, ambition
inspired and success achieved."*

Helen Keller

I recall that my perception of the relationship with Miles was "hellish"
and I wanted to get away from him. I felt like I was living a nightmare yet
the reality was that after Miles, I met James, the brother of the girl next
door. I got loads of sympathy and understanding, support not challenge.
I loved it, my addiction for support grew. James invited me to go down
to Buckinghamshire where he lived and begin a new life with him! I did.
I couldn't get there quick enough so I joined Lex Industrial Systems, part
of Volvo, as an Assistant Accountant, still pursuing my studies. My boss
there, Simon he was called, was lovely. I hid my past away and pretended
it did not exist. I was Lynn, who lived with James and was studying to be
an accountant. This sort of worked for me. I say sort of, because it was
a facade. The emotions of my grief and loss from the past kept on building
up inside, and on the outside I was lying. I kept putting a brave face on,
and now it was covering so many things. *You can run, but you can't hide,
eventually the unloved pain will find you, and you have to live and breathe it.*
I am so thankful to God for my challenge and pain. It is the most authentic

aspect of my life, that and recovering. If I only talk to others and share my experiences and insights, I will have lived a wonderful life, knowing that I am truly able to make a difference and help to stop unnecessary suffering.

Again, I appeared to be yet in another loop. James was very supportive of me but this actually began to turn me off him. It sounds so odd, doesn't it? A really respectable young man, honest and fun loving was turning me off by over-supporting me. I realise now that I needed to explore and understand myself more deeply and in new ways. I needed to know who I was and to overcome the trapped pain and misperception that I was carrying around in me and had been since I was a little girl. I know that now! I just did not know it then.

On an uplifting career note, I decided it was time to give up studying accountancy. I was more interested in how IT was helping businesses and enjoyed software implementation work. I had false pressure put on me to qualify as an accountant and the truth was that I actually did not enjoy the requirement of having to dress like an accountant in boring black, brown or navy suits. It was so old fashioned and rigid. One rebellious summer's day I turned up in a canary yellow suit. I mean the yellow was pretty rebellious in itself, but it was also the fact that I was not wearing a skirt or trousers, they were shorts. It certainly got the office talking and I had a big grin on my face.

At this point I decided to hand my notice in as I was going to return to the North of England however, my Boss convinced me to work as a contractor and implement a new software system. I was so capable in my work and everyone else seemed so dependent on me that I was able to increase my daily rates to such a ridiculous sum that in the end I felt "dirty" taking so much money. I truly believe in an honest day's work for an honest day's pay.

I had decided by that stage that I wanted to run my own business and undertake more software implementations. I could see that corporations needed expertise in implementing the new IT systems. I left Lex and worked for myself for three years until my second divorce came about and then I moved back North. This period of time was challenging but I don't recall feeling anxious or worried about how I was going to manage. I felt confident that I could do it. The hardest task was marketing, as I was weak in this area. Looking back I was a brave young girl and I learnt so much from the experience. Eventually it was getting harder to find work but I found a contract working for the Government's IT department on the Fylde Coast. It was a real eye opener into the world of government and what really goes on. For a while, I was satisfied putting my brave face on without telling anyone that I had been married and divorced not once, but twice. I felt I had to hide my failure. The more I hid my life however, the more I was setting myself up for more knocks because I was hiding the real underlying hurt of the loss of my sisters. I was hiding my divorces for fear of ridicule which would expose my pain. Whatever we repress eventually has to be expressed. I was only kidding myself that I was saving myself from more hurt.

After working for the government, I decided I wanted "proper" training in IT, and to work for an employer and provide myself with job security. The reality of running my own business saw me working extremely long hours. I had to wear about six or seven different hats. Feeling like a failure in my private life I wanted to prove that I was a success in my academic and business life and what better way was there to do this than vamp up my professional qualifications and prove to the world that I was an A-grader?

I decided to do a Master's Degree in Business Administration Information Technology around 1995. Not only that, but I also decided that nothing less than a distinction was acceptable so I worked jolly hard to achieve the perfection of a distinction. I proved that if you set your mind to something then it really is achievable but what I did not bargain for was that attaining a distinction and vamping up my qualifications did not mean it would solve all my inadequacy issues.

Once I got my Master's Degree I looked for the perfect global company to work for. I chose to work for Ford Motor. They employed experienced graduates and offered some of the best training around. This dream was soon punctured by working on an older technology project and getting a real feeling of how inflexible the organisation actually was behind the scenes. Why couldn't they let me follow my dream? In fact, my first Manager on a "soul" level tried to destroy my fantasies about the organisation, during which time I had a very difficult period of personal review. I was being tested by the Universe. I was so used to getting support and needing it, that when the going got tough, I was shocked that it was even happening. I stood my ground through two or three rounds of reviews, stating my grievance about how a manager could reduce an experienced accountant and a student with a distinction in a Master's Degree down to a trainee analyst who doesn't make the grade. Why had it come as such a shock to me? Surely the manager was supposed to be training me and letting me know where I was going off-course! After praying for divine intervention, the "trucking" vicar (as in ex truck driver turned Christian), my next door neighbour, advised me that so long as I knew in my heart that I was truthful, it didn't matter what they said about me. Oh, but it did and it hurt. After all, why was this man destroying my career so easily? I haven't worked The Demartini Method® on this manager yet, but I am sure now that when I do, I will find that he is a loving soul who had my interests at heart and he was building me up for my mission.

The balance in between the hard work was the fact that Ford had a great graduate community. I enjoyed skiing holidays, paragliding, outward bound courses and even a spectacular sailing holiday around the Caribbean Islands on a 46ft yacht, as well as joining the consultants from Logica on their sailing weekends across the Solent to France.

I left Ford after being headhunted by an agent seeking to recruit consultants for a software company. I handed my notice in to my manager who was disappointed. He had just agreed to pay for me to do a special business course only for Women at Cranfield; this was the equivalent of a $18K course and I was turning it down! Although I could not see it, I had great opportunities at Ford. I was allowing the incident with my manager to overshadow my judgment and I believed that the software company would be a more rewarding career option. It certainly turned out to be an enjoyable job role in which I travelled abroad and was challenged careerwise. The company ran into trading difficulties and so I jumped ship to avoid any potential layoffs or redundancies. The very thing I was trying to avoid, which was the loss of my job, was the key event in my next job. It was a new start up and involved a steep learning curve and the passing of numerous examinations. No sooner had we done all the hard work when we got the dreaded news that an American company, NCR, had taken over and no longer required an ecommerce division, so I was to lose my job for the third time.

You know the more often it happens to you the more prepared you are for it. It's not so much of a shock and in fact I have almost become expectant that it will happen—an American company will take over and either make your life miserable or fire you. Being made redundant can undermine a person's confidence, and is a big hit to the self-esteem because you feel unvalued and unwanted. You know that you are of value and it's not what it appears to be but still, it has a strong and powerful hit on your psyche. Not to mention the hard work ahead of you as you spend many hours searching for work and form filling, whilst also maintaining the depleting finances as best you can and taking care of the family as sole provider. Does it not all sound like a repeat of the loss, feelings of rejection, low self-esteem that I have been experiencing in my relationships?

Of course, there was another side to all of this, and The Demartini Method® showed me how the preparations and foundations were being laid out before me. My "yellow brick road" to over the rainbow is being painted on the landscape of life and you shall see the artist at work in all her fine glory. I've held out for a long time, obviously to build the story but it's starting to get like playing chicken now! I can't hold out for much longer. Trying to weather the effects as best as I can that my story is convincing for you is proving too hard.

Job losses did not appear to affect me in the early days but it was when I tried to begin a new life, mainly after my second divorce, and wipe the slate clean that I experienced from disappointment in my job roles. Clearly I was treating what had happened to me as "in the way and not on the way". This change in perception is vital if we are to use our so-called baggage as fuel to feed us and not drag us down. Through my lessons and experience I want to teach you how to do this.

CHAPTER 8

The Reality Of Motherhood

"Being a full-time mother is one of the highest
salaried jobs…since the payment is pure love."
Mildred B. Vermont

This chapter recounts the increased build-up by the Universe to awaken me to reality in motherhood. I experienced job loss and marriage loss whilst trying to nurture my baby. It was the amazing love for my child that provided me with the strength to get through each day, during this vulnerable phase of my life. Don't ever underestimate the power of love and how it is always there by your side if you know how to see it.

Despite my job losses, I was good at being able to find new roles in new companies. This time around Stuart and I had decided that we wanted to escape the busy rat race of outer London. I found my next role at Devon Valley Mill in the glorious fields of the Devon countryside. I had reached a juncture, job-wise. Did I want the joy of great salary rates, and an unfulfilling life fixed to a job? Or did living a family life mean more to me? Well, I chose a family life whatever I fantasised that to be. I did not want to be a slave to financial rates, yet at the same time money was important.

I took a job at the Mill and kind of unbeknown but knowing, I was pregnant at the time, I started work. I did feel rather guilty when I told my boss. He was lovely and accepted that fact. I was appreciative. For a while it worked and I was feeling fulfilled and supported in my job. I grew a big tummy but eventually they too axed my job after the Americans came and took over the company. They were lovely about that whole process, and to this day I feel thankful and grateful that when I was pregnant and worked for them, I had their full support. When we are working towards our mission, the Universe will take care of our needs and support will come from unexpected areas and doors open up.

There was a period of time when I thought that I was going to lose my baby. I was losing blood at four months and the Doctor had no explanation for it. I had to stay in bed. The Mill gave me 100% support which was truly wonderful and it totally counteracted the challenge I was facing with my partner. Thankfully, I got through this period, but I will never forget the love portrayed by the people at the Devon Valley Mill. They eventually made me redundant and were thoughtful enough to give me some redundancy pay even though legally they had no obligation to do so. I will never forget this. So I learnt that you can lose your job and it feels okay. I then moved to Devon County Council initially as a part time project manager. I was lucky enough to appreciate a part time contract that paid great rates. At this point in time I had left Stuart, my third husband, and my maternity period needed to come to an end. I was now a responsible single parent, so I placed Lauren with a child minder for two days a week. I was lucky to find Maureen, in Brixham. On the day I took Lauren to meet her she embraced Lauren and asked me to take a walk for half an hour. During that half an hour I was beside myself but when I got back to Maureen's, Lauren was fulfilled and fine! I felt safe leaving Lauren with her in the future, and to be perfectly honest it was the worst time in my life to be letting go of control of my daughter. Somehow the Universe was being kind and more than amenable to me... I was getting the support I needed. My role at Devon County Council was to grow and I took up a fulltime role as a Business Support Manager for their property department. When they went through some reorganisation I was promoted to an executive position as Business Manager responsible for all the business support services for the department. Things were good, yet at the same time they were extremely difficult. The divorce from Stuart was underway.

To say it was "difficult" is actually a gross understatement. Added to the divorce was the fact that I was embroiled in litigation with his mother over the marital home. I had trusted both Stuart and his mother only to find that I had got myself tied into a very onerous trust fund that meant I alone was fully responsible for paying the mortgage on a property that I would never own! Well, would I knowingly sign a document to allow this to happen? Yes, it is hard to appreciate and to comprehend, how I could be so absolutely trusting.

My life at this point felt like a living hell. I had two court cases on the go, plus social services involvement over Lauren. That was the private life booked up with stuff. At work I was dealing with a complete company restructure and yes it was a challenging job. At the time I worked harder and harder, and then eventually I began experiencing anger, anger like a volcanic eruption: you know the one that I had suppressed in my childhood. Funny that! Well it was funny looking back, I was angry at the sun for shining in my eyes, I was angry at a sign that said "Cycle to work and save fuel," I was angry at the wind for blowing my hair in my eyes. When I spoke to the doctor he said that I was suffering from stress and wanted to sign me off work. I refused to let him, I told him I had too much to do and get done, I didn't need time off! I needed more time! The doctor knew that a short time off work would see me curling up in a foetal position and needing to take the time out for recovery. I was off work for a while and when I returned my role had been taken over. My boss did not appear to me as supportive to say the least. It's a big chapter for another book so I won't dip into what happened.

What I can say is that I perceived my life to be a fight and a challenge. I felt like I was a victim. It hurt, I felt bruised, and I felt sad. I tried the best way I knew to fight on and protect my baby daughter from everything that was happening. The more I perceived myself as a victim the worse my victim situation got. Stuart was persistent in trying to see Lauren. Who could blame him for that? I felt it was too much for me and I involved the police, especially when I thought he might kidnap Lauren. It's a strange feeling when something you know as being one thing is reflected to you as something else. I felt like I was losing my mind. Was the world crazy? Well…there is always a balance somewhere in life and I have since learnt that physical events are not always what they appear to be

If I look for the balance in what was happening then I only have to look at the sailing trip to Torquay. My parents and I owned a Hanse sailing yacht and we had invited my friend Susan and her partner to sail from Brixham to Torquay. The wind was down so we were motoring and we had spotted a shoal of dolphins. I directed Dad to head towards them; we wanted a close up view. I was up at the bow and decided that I would call the dolphins in Dr. Doolittle style. Talking to the animals is something that I developed as a child and it was thrilling that they were responding by swimming under the boat; and they were big, I mean twelve feet in length at least. Suddenly, as I made special dolphin calls to them, one leapt up out of the water in front of me, it was face-to-face for a split second, I then fell backwards into the boat. I was shocked but delighted. My friend said that the dolphin was looking me right in the eyes. Afterwards we were amazed and calmly quiet in contemplation of the wonderful experience we had just had.

Dancing was another way in which I had balance in my life. Our dance school in Exeter put on a performance at the Theatre, it was without doubt a great pleasure to think that I was able to learn ballet and be part of a dance performance

As time progressed our family (Mum, Dad, myself and Lauren) applied to migrate away from the difficulties Stuart and I were having.

After spending a few years, all my spare time and limited money on litigation, lawyers and being in courts, I wanted to throw the towel in and find a new life free from all the difficulties. We decided that living abroad was the answer. We contemplated Spain and had taken a trip to Moraira where we had even looked at properties whilst we were there. I loved Spain—it was like a second home, and yet it didn't seem far enough away to feel protected. As a single parent, I simply couldn't survive working, receiving no maintenance and paying out for legal fees—it was just impossible. I was getting dragged down lower and lower until I would eventually hit rock bottom.

I left DCC and took a less onerous job whilst I navigated the Australian immigration system. My daughter was starting primary school and we had moved to a location away from where her father could find us, although we still had a lot of court dealings to attend to. I could not leave the UK without a Court Order granting permission and to do that I needed the agreement of her father who naturally would not want to do that. The path was a long and demanding one. I had to slowly and painfully go through the court procedures. The upside was that I learnt a lot about courts, solicitors, litigation, judges and the entire legal system in itself. In a nutshell, let me just share that it is advisable to stay away from legal situations: they will absorb a lot of finance and affect your emotional health. Justice is seen to be done, and that is it. The phrase "your day in court" does not necessarily mean you win your case and get what you perceive as justice. As I soon discovered during this time in my life, loss recurs in the form of financial loss too. It generated curiosity for me to see how many people in the world are grieving over the loss of not just family members, friends, jobs or loved ones, but also material wealth.

I'm curious to know what makes a person think that moving to another country allows them to escape their "stuff". Well, it helped me to avoid immediate litigation from Stuart. At least I was not in the divorce courts or child welfare, or spending time down at the solicitor's offices. And what effect does all this time away have on a career? Well, it makes it hard to focus on your career. Can you imagine that?

Once I had moved to Australia I put on my brave face at every interview and questioning process I went through. Funny that. My primary focus at the time was to get my daughter into school, and so I managed that. I thought it was best to then take a small casual job at first, not realising that casual actually and often means infrequent and unsteady. In the UK, casual means that you are at least guaranteed a fixed number of hours. You know a single mum needs a certain number of fixed hours to pay the bills. Some weeks they wanted me 25 hours and some weeks they wanted me four hours. How can anyone survive on four hours of paid labour? I found it difficult, however I am grateful for that experience of hardship, as yet again it has led to my mission and purpose in the world.

Eventually I met a great consultant from Data3, who located me some IT-related work in the cityat a company called Australian Water Systems. At the time it was a great start-up company that delivered water tanks to homes and businesses. The dams were at only 15% capacity at the time and so water was precious. I made some amazing friends that I still keep in touch with even now. The job was a short contract and, luckily, after the contract came to an end, I was able to find myself what I hoped was going to be a secure business analyst role at an Australian icon called Golden Circle. I was really pleased it was not too far to travel to work and so at last

I could feel more settled into the Australian way of life. Well, that sense of security lasted until Heinz Australia took over the organisation. Coming from the UK, I knew immediately what that meant; they wanted a leaner more efficient company with increased profit and it was not going to be about employee welfare.

At least I was not in the first round of redundancies—they wanted my skills to help them implement the business systems. The whole climate in the factory changed, and while I tried to shake it off, it just seemed to go from bad to worse. Firstly, the project I had successfully worked on and was on the point of implementing got canned. Then, I was given another complex and tricky project that did not have enough resources to continue its implementation. Meanwhile, the planned business system implementation was run in Melbourne and little information came out in Brisbane. About two weeks before the systems went live we were told to prepare for the pilot. I must say I was pleased with the resilience and persistence of the staff at the factory—they showed their full colours in the face of demanding expectations concerning the project. It was always difficult to gauge whether the management did not understand the impact, or whether it was part of the strategy to force people to leave on their own before they had to make redundancy payments.

I perceived that I was being treated badly and for that I was getting angry. I felt forced to tolerate the situation because of the pure fact that I needed to survive financially. The job agencies were not the easiest to understand and deal with. Some will call you back; some will allow you into the city for interviews, and some you never hear from again. The fear of losing my job and having great difficulty finding another one was exhausting. It's hard to describe the feeling when you need to be able to provide food and shelter for your offspring. I didn't have the luxury of child support. I chose not to pursue maintenance from Lauren's Father, all the way from Australia. Fair enough. I didn't want to rely on the State or anyone else—I wanted to be independent and successful.

It is hard at times to keep your head held up when things get tough. There is a fine line between being okay providing the basics and being out on the street. I am lucky that I had support around me and that I am both educated and extremely capable. I am fortunate that I have no debt problems, and that I have managed my money well. It may be frustrating that some Australian employers do not recognise English qualifications and experience but it's not as bad as not being recognised at all for being able to provide a service and earn money. It's also okay to say, "Think positive" or "What you think and thank about, you bring about," but when you are faced with adversity, maintaining those clear inspired thoughts becomes a struggle. Tell me, would you choose to walk in my path? If I had the choice of life stories, perhaps being a movie star is appears more appealing and a great pick for most people. My pick is the life I have lived, for I believe it is my mission to inspire others to resolve their emotional anguish and find possibility and hope where they feel there is none.

CHAPTER 9

Breaking Down Before Breaking Through

"Sometimes a breakdown can be the beginning of a kind of breakthrough, a way of living in advance through a trauma that prepares you for a future of radical transformation."

Cherrie Moraga

I would like to think that I was learning from all my situations. The truth is that yes, I have been learning but fundamentally, until now, I was unable to see the beauty and love that has been surrounding me 24 hours a day, seven days a week. I've just described what, to many, may seem like a life of loss and grief packed with repeated traumas so how could I possibly describe the love and beauty that was surrounding me? It sounds really bizarre, doesn't it? I would agree with you. In essence, I have pursued a repetitive path that has seen me experience loss to the extent that most people would have physically collapsed under it a long time ago, due to the sheer weight of the emotional baggage. What I have achieved is the certainty that I can say I am truly a master of loss. In being a master of loss, I too am a master of gain.

My brain has geared itself to reflecting and analysing life situations in an attempt to understand the "why" behind it all. I have outgrown and passed by many a friend because of my so-called 'analytical brain' that barely ever shuts off. They say, "Oh Lynn! Do you have to analyse everything?!" Well, I am proud of my analytical brain, it is not an ordinary brain and I believe part of my genius is my analytical ability. It has allowed me to see opportunities and find ways to transform myself through my situations, as well as being a fundamental part of my career in business. It also assists me enormously when I look at all the benefits and drawbacks while working through The Demartini Method®. I am awesomely appreciative of my active, thinking and analytical brain.

I have lived by what I now call the 40/40 rule: Dr J F Demartini has spent 40 years devoted to understanding human behaviour and building his work centred around The Demartini Method® (which you're about to be introduced to in the next Chapter so hold tight), and I have spent 40 years working myself up to the point of being ready for the method. Maybe that was meant to be so that the impact would be more powerful. The impact had to be powerful because it had to inspire me to write a book about all my mishaps. Who loves being that open writing a book is, in itself, a challenge and to write about personal emotional events that you have experienced in the past is even more challenging. If I can keep a lid on all that baggage to the extent that it would wear me down to utter exhaustion and breakdown, then I clearly have the strength to undergo a radical transformation, to put each one of these perceived traumatic events in its rightful place, in the past and in the context of my greater mission in life.

I can now share with you, in all honesty, how I successfully moved from being tired, worn out, and burnt out to having enough inspiration to begin working longer hours, working full-time as a single parent, and still manage to undertake research, study, and read books to continue to further my own evolution. On top of all of that, my life changed so dramatically that I have now written and published a book so that I can share my message and so that you can have another shot at life (if you've given up)—or if you are struggling to move past your loss and grief. If it sounds amazing, that's because it is.

I had visited my doctor on many occasions, and I had undergone various blood tests and other medical procedures to find out why I was so tired. There was never anything that showed up. I was stressed and not enjoying my life. At work, I was disempowered and faced blocks every way I turned. Everything appeared to be blocking my efforts to do a good job and succeed. Most of my time was spent outside of the present, living in either the past or dreaming of some vague future when it would all turn out all right. I knew there had to be a reason for the events in my life and I needed it to make more sense than simply saying, "I've made a lot of bad choices," because that is not how I view it. I made choices, most of them consciously and all of them according to what was most important to me at the time, and I have no regrets. I had experienced a lot of perceived emotional pain in my perception but surely there was a reason for it all, a purpose. I was more and more disheartened with life and I had to find the reason why I was here. I could not tolerate what seemed to be constant struggle anymore; all roads always ended with enormous effort and despair. This was making me even more tired.

The pain barrier, or rather the pain threshold, of a human being is tremendous and people will go through an enormous amount of it before they will be moved to action. I thought my pain barrier was low in myself and it appears to be so, physically. However, emotionally I have endured such repeated, extreme losses that other people might have found them to be unbearable. I think that pain comes before the creation of new forms. Certainly the Universe is evolving and the experience of pain speeds up that process. There has to be death before new life, pain comes with pleasure and loss signifies the arrival of gain. You have to give up and let go of what was in order to move to what is. As humans, we struggle with that and we try to fight our own growth instead of stepping through and up to embody a new quantum of life.

I had really struggled with letting go. I knew my sisters were dead but religion aided me to hold onto them for longer, to the extent that I fantasised about being able to bring them back to planet earth. I did not want to let go of them but interestingly I did go for some psychotherapy only to be told that I had not let go of them. I was taken through a process whereby I said goodbye to them, by writing them a letter and finding a beautiful spot where I could leave it. I followed the process and felt good about it, yet I still had a nagging feeling about how could I let go of something that is always there. My sisters may be dead and I know that they will not appear again in front of me in their physical form, but I do know that they live on as souls of the Universe.

I have been going through 40 years of revisiting that loss in many different ways. Clearly, after the death of my sisters the resultant traumatic effect was etched on my mind and body and without therapy of any kind, the trauma would need to repeat itself until I began to learn the lessons and balance it out. As I mentioned before, Dr J F Demartini teaches that whatever we have not learned to love, will be repeated until we love it. It was clear that I needed to love the loss—in my family life, in my work life, and in my personal life—and know that nothing was really missing at the time that I perceived the loss.

There were various points in my life where I tried to seek help and support or further my knowledge and understanding—but clearly they did not work too well at the time. I recall going to the doctor in my late teenage years. I was trying to recognise that I was experiencing depression, but he just said to me that what I was experiencing was normal daily life. I went to a different doctor to explore why my energy levels were so low, he just talked about how great his wife was, she could work, run a home and do loads of stuff. During the failure of my second marriage I was simply prescribed drugs. They didn't really do anything as far as I could tell and I had no confidence in drugs; to me it was obvious that I might feel down after what I had experienced.

I began reading as a means of learning and understanding however, back then there was no Internet or Amazon bookstore and so there was no easy or immediate access to some of the wonderful self-help literature that is around now. My mother, bless her, gave me a book on the stages of grief and this at least helped me to feel that I was a normal person and that these strong emotions and feelings were okay. At last, someone recognised and could explain with some accuracy what I was experiencing. The book was written by Elizabeth Kubler-Ross. Another friend, Paula, owner of a designer curtain shop in Lytham gave me a book to read called *The Precious Present* and that gave me a great means of holding onto my life. Quite frankly, whilst I knew I would never commit suicide, I simply felt that there was nothing worth living for. On the one hand I can't believe that I felt that low, and that I actually thought like that but on the other hand, I am not at all surprised I felt like that. Many people do and at times they can feel worse and even attempt a suicide. As a fellow human being I feel it is my job to help prevent anyone from finding they are lost with nowhere to go.

My book is part of a promise to begin a career that will serve to help others through difficult times. If I can make just one life matter then my authentic work and mission will be realised.

I remember reading Louise Hay's Book, *The Power is Within You*. After reading of her own traumas in early childhood, I was able to relate to how she no longer wanted to tolerate her situation and began taking steps to get out herself out of that way of life. The book certainly inspired me further and gave me a stronger conviction to make the emotional pain mean something more beneficial, more creative and more rewarding. I did not want to be a victim all my life.

My third marriage was a great precipitator in depleting my energy and bringing me to a saturation point. I really had tried everything to make that marriage work. I recall after the third marriage failure, my husband agreed to come to *Relate*, the agency which supports relationship issues. There are two things etched on my mind: one is the fact that after telling her about the death of my sisters, she kind of laughed (yes, I know this might sound odd, but it's what she did) and then basically she said I was programmed after that to be a victim. I felt awful. Despite that, I pursued a course of counselling with my husband. We adopted her advice on a strategy to prevent arguments from escalating out of control but they failed. The verbal signal was for me to say "Give me some space." This was a trigger to mean, "I need time out." The way I said it triggered him though. Our counsellor gave up on us both and said there was nothing more she could do. I recall feeling helpless and devastated. I would rather have heard the words, "Lynn, you are living in a fantasy and this is the necessary pain to break it so you can live a more meaningful and fulfilling life in the long-term."

After leaving Stuart, it was a couple of years before I moved into my own place again. I had lived at Mum's with Lauren as a baby. By then the Lauren-seeing-Stuart arrangements were working okay, although I was always present during visits. Once I moved, it wasn't long before I allowed Stuart to charm his way into our lives again, only to find that I closed off contact once again to cut a long story short, I perceived Stuart's continued attempts to see Lauren as unwanted and eventually I called the police to help. It was then that I sought help from a group who supported women who perceived that they were experiencing marital issues. That was an eye opener! After the course I opted for further counselling. I was then able to recognise why I had tried repeatedly to make the relationship work, when it could not. I failed to see my part in the whole equation. I eventually stopped Lauren's contact with her father, as I perceived the situation to be unsuitable for her.

As helpful as it was, what was I to do? How was I going to pick my life up? I felt like a complete dropout and was imagining all sorts of negativity; I'm single, divorced and no respectable people would want to associate with me. After all, a single woman is a threat, I might want their husbands. Single friends seemed like a good option, but then I was unable to go for night's out—I had a baby to look after. There was no way that I would let anyone look after Lauren, I trusted no-one. How could I trust another person when I wasn't trusting of her father?

I was separated from everyone—and this was the beginning of a long period of solitude, like a prison sentence, where I would spend many years in a dark phase. It was a period of change so profound that at times it was impossible to see the light at the end of the tunnel. I felt there would never be one, however I had learnt that there really was no way out. I had to live it and learn to live it as enjoyably as I could. I did not realise that I had imprisoned myself!

So I went through a period of trying to control absolutely everything. I figured that if I was ultra-careful, then I could stop more pain and my life might just about be liveable. Have you ever felt like this? Are you so controlling that nothing is allowed to happen without your permission? It's sad sometimes when life has to get that way. And so many people talk about it like a person is the "pits" to be doing that and behaving in that way. Well guess what, I understand it and it's not so terrible. It's understandable when you consider what has happened in that person's life! Do you hear what I am saying? Only when you have experienced such solitude can you even begin to embrace and understand the love that is all around you in the world.

My breaking point was being reached; the doctor could not find anything physically wrong with me. Work was becoming a source of great anger, and I felt I could not keep the lid on the anger. It was only a matter of time before something was going to explode. Eventually there would be an expression of the suppression. My voice has been small for all these years, a kind of experiencing in silence, however I cannot do it anymore and I want others to know that they do not have to do it anymore. It was a friend of mine who suggested that I seek out a change in perceptions and recommended that I attend The Breakthrough Experience® with Dr. John Demartini, which is his signature weekend program that he runs all over the world today—more than 30 times every year. The next chapter describes what I discovered at The Breakthrough Experience®.

CHAPTER 10

The Breakthrough Experience®

*"The Breakthrough Experience® is the most valuable
gift of a lifetime, as it allows you to experience the
precious present and the truth of love."*

Lynn Hope Thomas

Moving from the United Kingdom to Australia was to be a new start for me, a new life. Little did I realise just how marvellous the move would be. It was an exciting move from the aspect of living in a new country and enjoying what the country had to offer. I certainly had no idea that it would be the start of a radical transformation that would begin in the often sunny and laidback city of Brisbane, Australia.

I arrived in Australia believing that there was going to be a strong demand for the skills I had acquired in the field of IT. That was just a fantasy, a fantasy of leaving Britain behind and coming to a country where I would end up being a "legal alien" and not an "in demand" person. I was fortunate enough to find Mark Landells from Data3. I worked for Australian Water Systems as a contractor, and soon realised that Australia was different from the UK in terms of the labour market… clearly, I had been spoilt in the United Kingdom without ever knowing it.

Australian Water Systems was a lovely organisation to work for. To this day, I am grateful to Mark for finding me the job that introduced me to the

Australian market. I was to make some very strong friendships there. We have had lots of laughs and fun together. It was wonderful after what I had recently experienced in the UK. One of these great friends, Daniela Stalling, introduced me to the works of Dr J F Demartini. It was odd in a way: she simply said that she thought I was 'ready' for it and that Dr J F Demartini was able to offer a new perspective on how situations could be viewed. That was all she said, and because of her certainty and inspiration, I believed her every word. Naturally, I booked in for the course. The weekend booking cost for The Breakthrough Experience® would cost me around $1500 but if Daniela said it was worth my time and investment, then I believed her. She was going on the same course and we would go together.

We booked accommodation in the hotel where the event was happening. Daniela explained to me that the days would be long and we would need to get as much sleep as we could. How true this was and still is! I always recommend a solid night's kip before and after a Demartini event. I laugh now, because I reckon everyone who has ever been would make the same recommendation. We arrived and registered really early, like 8.00am or something, and there was such a great buzz in the room. I felt excited to see lots of people from all backgrounds and walks of life, looking motivated and keen for the upcoming two days. There was a great sense of excitement and some kind of magical feeling in the room.

The show then hit the road! John began talking. It was encapsulating, mesmerising, intriguing; I mean, you lapped up every word he uttered. I did not want to go to the toilet or risk missing one single word. I can now say that I've been to many Demartini events and I feel the same every time. I do not want to miss a single word of his. Of course at some point I do need a bathroom break but I hate going.

John is a star performer. Yet, it's actually more than that, as what he says is so important. *How* he says it is so important. All his words are designed just for YOU to hear and understand and change your life with. Talk about lighting up the spirit and engaging people. John's teachings change and transform lives, wake people up and bring them to brand new, deep and extraordinarily profound realisations about their lives— and what they are here on the planet to do and to fulfil. After 40 years of being tangled in emotional agony, John's words were like manna to my heart… like a healing remedy after so many years of struggle. Yet, I was not the only one in the room, there were another 100 maybe 200 similar souls wanting to absorb his every word. I'd attended a lot of good corporate training courses, but I had never experienced one that was anything like this. John kept telling us that he would not leave the room until each person had experienced what he called a "breakthrough". I think I left the room at around 12.30am and there were still people needing to break through. He certainly was true to his word.

The first day is an account of the "science" behind The Demartini Method® and then around the first late afternoon, we all begin to undertake the method on an emotional charge of our choosing. Mine was dead easy to pick—it was my ex-husband and the key traits I was emotional about were my perceptions that he had been dishonest, lied and perceived that had used my identity I was so adamant that I was a very honest person with integrity that I even asked John about it. I said, "I can't think of situations where I would lie." He looked at me firmly with his eyes and said, "Yes, you lie. Now start thinking of when you have lied." I recall protesting. He swore firmly at me and basically told me to get on with it. I thought long and hard and eventually I began to recall lies that I had told, to different people throughout my life and in different ways. As I progressed through the method, I could see that I was dishonest and told lies and that I rationalised these events as serving a purpose. I had justified the lying as being "good" and okay. Really, who am I to judge another for things that I do myself? Eventually the tears of appreciation came as I realised, during the method, that I had harshly judged my ex-partner, and that really, he was waking me up to the denial I had put myself through and to the fantasy that I was holding onto. This was a truly amazing method. It really shifted my perspective and I was humbled but emotionally I felt like a weight had been lifted off me. Now this might have seemed amazing enough but it didn't stop there.

Next, after we had broken through our misperceptions, John asked us to find a person in the room who reminded us of the person that we had done The Demartini Method® on. We were then instructed to sit down opposite them and share our realisations, unconditional love and new perspective on their presence in our lives.

As I looked around for my ex-husband in the room a lady wanted me to represent her mother. I was confused: how could I represent her mother if I did not know her? There must be some mistake. As we sat down opposite each other, a facilitator in The Demartini Method® took us through the process. I sat patiently and listed as the lady opened up her heart and spoke to me. I was her mother who had passed away 10 years previously. As she spoke her words to her mum, I instantly recognised that she was really a reflection of me, saying what I needed to say to my mum. I know it sounds bizarre but it was like magic happening before my eyes. I felt even more tears come to my eyes. She said how she had misunderstood her mum and not listened to her mother's values, and that in doing so, she had felt unloved. When it came to my turn to speak, I put my arms around her and hugged her close. I wept as I told her how I had loved her from the moment I had set eyes on her at birth. We embraced for several moments, both weeping—not with sadness but with comprehension of a deep unconditional love that made the rest of the room disappear. I knew that my mum loved me and I also knew that what I had to do was change my misperception.

This unexpected, synchronous and spontaneous experience deeply impacted my psyche because what had happened was so magical: it was like being let into the secret garden, or like passing through a time warp. No words can adequately express how much I appreciate the experience and the impact it has had on my life.

Next, I had to pick out my ex-husband and my eye caught Martin, a guy my friend and I had been speaking to, and who sat behind us in the room. Was it him? No, it didn't feel right but then I saw him, another gentleman who had the demeanour of my ex. When I began explaining to him how my husband had betrayed me, he said to me, "No, I would never do that to my wife." It's funny, but I found his words upsetting. Why was he talking about himself and his wife? It wasn't working the method and there was no revelation. I looked to the facilitator for guidance and afterwards, I dwelled on it.

It really got to me. I obsessed over it for a few days after the weekend had come to a close. I even tried to track down the facilitator and ask her if she knew what had happened. It was later that I rationalised the experience myself. This guy was so similar to Stuart in that there was no way he could or would accept that he might do anything 'wrong' to me. His focus was purely on himself, in my perception, and he had no ability to consider another person. I felt relieved and grateful for the experience. The process was working after all—it was a blessing.

During the next few weeks my brain was trying to cope with the whole experience. It was buzzing and full of light. Ideas were popping in and out. It was like fireworks at times. Mostly this would happen at night whilst I was sleeping, I would then wake up in the middle of the night and be thinking through what I needed to do next, asking what my mission was, how it would take shape and form. It is really hard to get across to you just how amazing this experience was. My brain buzzed. For the first time I could feel all the electrical flirtations hitting each cell! The release of energy was amazing. Suddenly, during the day I was more energetic, I could apply myself to more things. I did not feel that I was wasting my time… for the first time I felt purposeful. I returned to my doctor and to the psychologist and told her that I didn't need her any more. She showed surprise in her expression. She asked me a series of questions and I answered each one with certainty and clarity. She was convinced and offered me the chance to revisit her and give her an update. I told her that I had more energy, I was revitalised, and that I now had a mission worth working towards because my energy was renewed. I was going to set up a business and continue with this remarkable method. She smiled and wished me luck. She said she wanted to hear that I had done what I said. She left me her number and said that I could call her at any time if I so needed. I have never needed her since but I so intend to call her.

I am so grateful to her for her lovely work and approach with me. She never gave me the impression that I was "ill" needed "treatment" or that anything was ever really wrong with me. When I told her what I would be doing, she was supportive and made no comments that could pull me back down. She allowed me to be me. As soon as this book is published I want to visit her and tell her how well I have performed by following The Breakthrough Experience®. When I saw the doctor, she too was sceptical; maybe cautious is a more accurate word. I have not had to visit the doctor for more than two years now! That is remarkable After a couple of weeks, lies and more lies kept rising to the surface. Each time they did I realised that John Demartini was right. I was a big liar. As they arose, my appreciation for The Demartini Method® grew and continues to do so. It is amazing how the human mind can bury the truth

Even as I read back the message I am trying to get across to you, somehow it fails to do it justice. How do I explain to you the enormous impact that working The Demartini Method® has had upon me? Maybe the next Chapter, *Chapter 11: After The Breakthrough Experience®*, will begin to show you how the work permeated my life and has continued to do so ever since that first attendance at The Breakthrough Experience®. What I hope is that you will get a taste of how the method can benefit you. It is not just about dissolving emotions, it has the power to truly transform your life into a more fulfilling one by allowing you to do what you love and love what you do.

CHAPTER 11

After The Breakthrough Experience®

"You can't connect the dots looking forward; you can only connect them looking backwards. So you have to trust that the dots will somehow connect in your future. You have to trust in something—your gut, destiny, life, karma, whatever. This approach has never let me down, and it has made all the difference in my life."

Steve Jobs

My wish for you is to see the transformation that occurred in me following The Breakthrough Experience®. If I can connect and inspire you to experience it, then imagine what can become of your life. My looking backwards at the dots was cloudy but following The Breakthrough Experience® I knew that I was experiencing what they call 'enlightenment'—I felt unbelievably enlightened by the experience. The enlightenment seemed to continue every night for a further two to three weeks. My brain felt like it was lighting up with fireworks as the realisations about Universal Laws and aspects of human behaviour continued to occur. I could almost feel the flow of blood through my neural pathways, sprouting ideas and completing other illusions of the past. First, I began to talk to people at work about The Breakthrough

Experience®. I started out carefully, simply because I was conscious that the concepts are challenging. It wasn't that what I'd discovered was so left field, it was that I knew I had been introduced to a completely new way of living—like Dr J F Demartini says, "A new and refreshing paradigm and perspective on life"—and without the same experience that I had on the weekend, it may come across completely out of context. At first I was running a fine line between the strong desire to share the deep and profound discoveries that had already changed my life and realising just how extraordinary my experience had been.

I began to adhere to the principles and apply The Demartini Method® whenever I encountered an extreme emotion or life issue. My thought process and thinking was really changing, as I viewed every situation from a different angle. My levels of attention and energy were significantly changed. At work I was experiencing difficulty when communicating with my boss. If you recall Heinz had taken over Golden Circle and redundancies were rife. He was based in another city, I rarely saw him and I knew that since the takeover they wanted all support roles to be operated out of Melbourne. The fear of losing my job and struggling as a single parent did not prevent me from doing my best. The harder I tried to show my boss that I knew what I was doing and was good at it, the more I perceived that he was downgrading me. I would get angry and stressed. My energy levels would be affected, and my mind was constantly battling the running of a complex project with limited resources while trying to watch my back, then coming home and being supportive to my daughter. I detested being in this position of vulnerability.! was so sick of the struggles which I felt I had been battling year after year. Things had to change.

I was invited by *Global 1 Training* to attend a one day workshop with Rowan Burn (a facilitator in Dr J F Demartini's work) which was free. So yes, following the breakthrough which was held over a weekend, I was now devoting more weekend time to personal development. If you remember, I had started off being too tired to even take the dog for a walk! That day proved to be rewarding. Rowan went over a few key principles from Dr J F Demartini's work, in particular a piece of work on fear and how it blocks you from moving forward. On that Sunday, using Rowan's advice, I unblocked the fear of losing my job. It was incredibly liberating to let go of it and know that whatever happened would be okay, no matter what. I went to work on the Monday and had a kind of eureka moment when my boss called and said that he needed me to work in the business on a more pressing issue. I thought, why would he do that if I was about to be made redundant? To me at the time, I had let go of the fear of losing my job and in my mind I felt that this was a connection to having done the work on fear! The project I had been working on was riddled with problems and it was a blessing to be offered a new piece of work.

I was much more fulfilled in my role at work following the work I had done on fear. I was more relaxed and less anxious. I still worked hard, although I did not enjoy my perceptions of how I was being treated at the time but I have new perspectives on it now. I knew that working in this environment was not my true mission and the reason it stressed me so much and made me angry, was the Universe letting me know that I needed to change what I did. The truth was that I was not doing what I loved. It was just a job. However, I was able to take the anger and convert it into a determination to succeed in my own business. The anger was giving me fuel to succeed at something else. I was grateful for the anger; I was now appreciative of the way I was being treated.

When I was called into the office with HR and my boss, I knew what was coming—my redundancy. I was balanced, poised and present. At last the Universe was giving me a strong message, and an undeniable confirmation that it was time for me to pursue my mission. Despite their concerned looks when they told me that I had lost my job, I simply smiled and said, "Thank you…don't look so worried, I am okay." Eureka yet again! Can you imagine being a single parent, with no maintenance or alternative source of income, saying thank you for being made redundant? You see, the beauty of The Demartini Method® is that you know that there are no mistakes to be found in the way life unfolds. An ending is a new beginning, a loss is the end of a cycle and the gain will present in a new form. I knew with certainty from the method that my life would gain from this loss. I knew it was a process that had to be followed. I knew that whilst I could not necessarily see how the gain would present in my life, I knew it would be there.

I had learnt from Dr J F Demartini that growth occurs on the border of both support and challenge. So the support of the redundancy would be met by a challenge. Just because the Universe had got me a redundancy, did not mean that suddenly everything was going to fall into place. My challenge now was how I was going to get off the ground. It is one thing to dream but it's another to truly manifest the dream. It takes work, dedication, focus, persistence and above all, a strong, strong reason to do it. It has to mean everything to you—and be what you believe you are here for, the thing that you were destined to do. I had vague ideas on how I was going to make it real, and now the vagueness was so real. I learned very quickly that vagueness is not enough to survive—you are required to be very clear, precise and with a specific targeted plan. The clearer you are, the clearer you are to your marketplace, and the clearer your marketplace will be on what service you are offering.

Working on a new way forward would take clarity and planning. I had several aims I wanted to achieve. Firstly, I wanted to get the proper organisational structure to process my work through. I wanted to build a website to connect and network. I wanted to learn more about presentational work and of course I wanted to write a book about the whole experience because I wanted to tell people who needed help where to come and find it.

Among all these desires I was also full of inspiration which was having a dramatic effect on my activities; I was working fast and furiously. I wanted to achieve great things as I have been working on doing ever since I first attended The Breakthrough Experience®. I set out a six month plan, initially with six key activities and I ensured that I got them done. Basically I set up a website, a company, got business cards, researched venues, considered marketing material, and held my first public talk. It felt great and I learned so much from all of the experiences. Of course there were challenges and I had to be persistent and overcome them, but it did eventually get easier.

The second six months were very much focussed on attending The Demartini Method® Training Program ™ and the Prophecy 1 Experience ™ course which allowed me to further explore and understand The Demartini Method®. I can say without hesitation that my first experience, whilst enormously powerful, was indeed just a taste of the continued powerful influences that were to come from other personal breakthroughs, from listening to other people's stories and from witnessing the effects that Dr J F Demartini has had on people who experienced a perceived loss in any area of their lives. I have no qualms about standing on a soap box and declaring to people the marvels of the method. In the first year I worked on my own presentation material, booked a room and got advertising in place. All of these things presented challenges and I thought my first presentation would never come about. I was grateful to my friend who agreed to help on the night, despite being hopelessly in love. Let's think about it, help on a Demartini presentation or spend time with a guy you are in love with? She chose to work with me! And so did my lovely mum, who dressed up beautifully for the occasion.

The evening was a wonderful experience for me. I got to practice my presentation skills and deliver the material I had worked hard on. I overcame my big fear of doing the presentation and I had received feedback from my audience which was good. Better yet, was when my own mother said to my dad, "I thought Lynn did really well, I never knew she could do anything like that!" This was the gem of all gems! In my perceptions I had always believed that I couldn't do anything very well. Can you see the change? My first night working on presenting my experience of The Demartini Method® to the public was enjoyable and gave invaluable rewards. I am grateful to my friend who assisted me and proposed some marketing ideas for my presentations. It's amazing don't you think, that from being tired and worn out I had now become so totally inspired?

Very soon I was able to run employment contracts through my new company setup to bring support and greater effectiveness and efficiency to individuals and businesses This was good news. It also led me through a variety of challenges surrounding insurance, operating procedures, finance and legalities. At times I felt like I was living my life by the skin of my pants! With too much to do, limited time to do it in and limited financial resources, I quickly became anxious. To compensate for the feeling of not having enough time I ensure my morning ritual happens. I thank the Universe, I watch the sky for signs, and I appreciate all that is happening in my life, I breathe deeply; I practice yoga and walk my dog for exercise. I repeat this at the beginning and end of the day and it works a treat.

Working this method has had great results for me. I continue the practice daily and never give up on it. I have found that in work situations if I come across conflicts or issues, I can use The Demartini Method® to collapse the situation and resolve the issue. There are too many traits to mention in this book but suffice it to say that each time I work the method the knock on results provide balance and smooth running in my life and have taught me things that could have taken years to discover. I have become a master of change and having had such a lot of it in my life I know with certainty that I can offer insight into how to embrace change and let go of old habits and limiting thoughts.

As individuals, we will often lie to ourselves if we are not ready to face the truth and I am as guilty of doing that as the next person. I do like to think though that I am beginning to live a more authentic life by balancing my emotions and not allowing my vision to be distorted by my perceptions. I have read that the ego gets very upset if we try to peel back its veil and reveal its big cover ups. I know this personally and I now expend a lot more energy in letting the ego fade so that I can allow myself to see the true love flowing all around me. I also trust what is happening and know that I don't have to fight it. I know that the Universe may present a challenge and I can trust that it is what the Universe knows is best for me. Letting go and letting it happen is the easiest path to take.

The above point didn't come easily to me and I was presented with a few scenarios in the year to really learn the lesson; I was made redundant once lost my contracts twice. I was grateful and thankful each time however, the depth of gratitude had really kicked in by the third time. The benefits of those situations were supporting the writing of this book as the Universe was giving me the time to write, focus and have a big push of determination to be persistent and complete it. The task of writing a book does seem pretty intimidating at first, and I can see why not everyone is writing a book. It's true that you need to have a mission and message. I feel that I am now on my mission, so I am not going to stop, give up or turn around, I am going to bulldoze my way through and take any adversity on the chin. Starting the book was a journey for me because I did not really know what I might discover as I began to pull apart the story of my life. I know that the earlier chapters required great strength to actually get the words out because of the painful memories buried in layers. As I have been writing, these feelings have been surfacing and so I have needed to deal with them. This time however, I have a great tool to assist me with any strong emotional charges and of course I have used mentoring to help as well. It's also useful to write the diary comments as I progress through the writing of the book, as I feel that these give further depth to the new journey I am on. They also give you, the reader, an opportunity to understand the broader perspective of the scientific tool and the effect it can have upon your life.

It would certainly appear to be the case that, had I been able to find The Demartini Method® sooner, I might have avoided some of the heartaches that I went through and become more enlightened—more aware—sooner. I think the "Que sera sera" fits well; whatever will be, will be. It wasn't for me to learn any sooner, I had to experience the effect of my emotions to the extent I did. Why? Well, because it's part of my spiritual path which, I hope, puts me in a position of understanding of so many aspects of people's lives that they are grappling with.

Dr J F Demartini says that his method has a thousand uses—and I think that is modest. I can see a whole impact on the corporate industry that will support the leading organisations for the next 100 years. Companies will be able to improve on their levels of efficiency instead of exasperating the levels of stress. They will be able to promote a healthier workforce and higher productivity using this scientific method. I spent many, many years reading self-help books. It has been slow progress yet that is perfect as it has given me the opportunity to master my work and now that I have found The Demartini Method®, I am equipped with a much speedier tool to support my life.

The time after The Breakthrough Experience® has been very transformational and, indeed, an awakening to a level of consciousness I never had previously. It's a level of consciousness that makes life authentic, beautiful and magical. My entire life story that you are now very familiar with, is a true example of not only how unresolved emotions can stop you in your path—and block you from your mission—but also of the radical transformation that is possible when applying The Demartini Method® to overcome challenges. If I can find new inspiration for life again after losing my twin sisters, being made redundant on numerous occasions and enduring three divorces among other financial losses, then you can find blessings in your own losses too.

I have loved sharing my story with you, and I hope that you have a new awareness that Universal balance is all around you, just as it was throughout all my earlier perceived traumas. I have found my mission after 40 years. It's joyful to know that I am consciously on track now. It means that I can be more authentic with the people I meet; I can help people to break through the barriers that prevent them from doing something amazing with their lives—something which I have always wanted to do. Above and beyond all of this, it means that I can appreciate the presence of God within and all around me.

CHAPTER 12

Time for You to Love Loss

"Mostly it is loss which teaches us about the worth of things."
Arthur Schopenhauer

For years I had been hiding inside my loss and grief without knowing there was a reason for it in my life. I had no appreciation for the presence of loss, mostly because I didn't understand the purpose of it in my life. And, as you have seen, it repeated in virtually all areas of my life and each time the perceived emotional pain grew stronger because each time I was trying to run from it. Pain is inevitable in life and it's a part of our growth however, we can use The Demartini Method® to love what we have pushed away.

Unbeknown to me, until March 2010 when I attended The Breakthrough Experience®, I have always been on my mission. I recall having a glimpse at the age of 14 that I wanted to help people. It stemmed from the inner child who perceived that she had no support at the time of the death of her sisters. It had created a great amount of compassion in me for the sufferings of others and a feeling that I wanted to help relieve their pain. When my mentor at the time, Rowan Burn, took me through the loss of my sisters using The Demartini Method®, I found it to be more effective than any other therapy or self-help book I'd ever read or experienced.

Rowan Burn is a mentor who has had his own personal amazing experience of turning his life around. It was his experience of transforming his own loss into a gain that undoubtedly benefited me. Thank you Rowan, the results were both deeply inspiring and highly motivational. I felt complete peace about the deaths of my sisters. I felt that they had given me a great gift by putting me in the spotlight without having to compete to be authentic. I felt fortunate. It did not take away the event that had happened in my life, but it certainly changed my perspective and outlook in a remarkable way. It lifted any charges that were dulling my energy and brain waves and helped to re-energise my body ready for my mission.

Since working with Dr J F Demartini as a facilitator in The Demartini Method®, I have had the opportunity to witness Dr J F Demartini taking other people who have experienced loss through The Demartini Method®. Every time, without fail, they have been released from their grief and have a new understanding and level of comprehension that is both inspiring and heart-opening. You can read the account from Adrian Virgo of her recent experience, as she was taken through her loss. I also witnessed a doctor in Brisbane being transformed through the same process. I met her some eight months later and asked her about her experience. She said it was the best thing for her and that while she still experienced the loss of her husband she had been less emotional and more accepting of it and could see the benefits that had transpired since the loss and since the breakthrough. Just to clarify, The Breakthrough Experience® explains the science behind the work and covers Side A and Side B. Dr J F Demartini chooses a member of the audience to take through a Side C. It is one of the most remarkable transformations of perception that can be witnessed.

As a trained facilitator I take clients through the Side C process. It requires experience and training to be able to get the best for clients. It has taken me 40 years to get to this point. It is with all that experience behind me that I can confidently write this book. I know with certainty and presence that my message will help many people. I invite you to contact me if you know in your heart that you need help to uncover whatever aspects of your loss are holding you back. I recall the humbleness I felt when I helped a lady to cry for the first time after four years over the loss of her husband; and to see her a year later I can see how her whole physiology has changed.

For me the words written by Marianne Williamson and can be looked up for full detail at http://www.marianne.com/ speech ring so very true:

"Our deepest fear is not that we are inadequate,

Our deepest fear is that we a

Please visit the website and read the rest of the words which are truly inspiring.

I am now consciously choosing to allow my light to shine through. I would love to reach out and touch the hands and hearts of those who are affected by loss and lead them through this magnificent and authentic transformation methodology. If you do the work and practice this method, new possibilities open up in your life, as they have been in my life. The Breakthrough Experience® has a solution that can permanently resolve many emotionally intense feelings, both good and bad, and resolve any action or inaction you wish to master, that can be either in you or another person. Loss is also a common instance on Programmes and projects of work, Corporations can significantly benefit from unlocking the blocks that key staff holds onto during the lifecycle of projects. Again this is something I have experienced in the large corporations where I have worked.

You saw in the previous chapters what the results of my work were using the method on my own experiences. My story was full of 'loss'—each one affecting me deeply and limiting my successes in life—but when the true light of love was shone, it revealed a beautiful, love-filled mission, not to mention my determination to fulfil it. For you, my entire life has provided an example of how you can shine light on any loss. Working through so many losses I am now an expert at loss transformation. You will benefit from what is revealed during the process, as it is amazing and wonderful. I intend that you will be inspired to take steps to look at your loss and what it may be revealing to you. Remember what you don't learn to love now, will repeat itself as sure as "eggs are eggs".

In this chapter, I want to share with you some of the changes that have happened since I followed the advice of Dr J F Demartini and began to write my dreams for life down on paper. In reading it, I want you to focus and imagine what could happen for you too, if you take time to thank and think about what you would love to see happen in your life, whether in your personal life or your business and career.

For those who have experienced the loss of a loved one, a job, a marriage, a relationship or even a large financial sum of money and you're struggling to cope with your emotions then the first thing you will learn is the truth about grief. It is the withdrawal symptom from a trait, or action that the person did or does that you are infatuated with. Whether you admit it or not the truth is that you are infatuated with (in differing degrees) to traits or actions regarding the person, job, marriage, relationship or situation regarding the money that you 'miss'. You may have been experiencing a high degree of pride and the loss was sent by the Universe to wake you up and humble you to see the beauty of life. Think about this; there will definitely be aspects of every person or situation that you dislike—and it's not possible to grieve over the loss of something you dislike, wouldn't you agree?

Side C of The Demartini Method® assists you in identifying all of the traits that you like and dislike and shows you how these have now been taken on by a different person or people in your life. You learn that nothing is ever missing. You learn that your loved one is around you—or that your financial loss has transformed itself to another form of wealth. The grief can be dissolved. The emotions you may be dealing with disappear and you will feel gratitude and love.

As a facilitator, I have gone through many hours of training with Dr J F Demartini always adding to the number of amazing transformations witnessed and experienced. Although the questions on the forms are simple it does require guidance and that is where my expertise in the method lies. My experience guides you through the process and ensures that you truly capture all the aspects that will bring about a transformation in your perceptions. On top of all of this, The Demartini Method® has also allowed me to consider all areas of my life and think about what goals I want to set and what I want in my life.

Spiritual—Your Expression

The Demartini Method® will bring you your first experience of true Universal synchronicity and the ability to see that you are surrounded by love all of the time—24/7—and that you cannot escape from it. Depending on what your beliefs concerning spirituality are, the method will expand your understanding of your soul and can help you find your inner voice, a sense of purpose and how to find your authentic self.

Spiritually, I have opened up to see the magnificent beauty of God's expression within the Universe. The method is designed to show you the remarkable synchronicity that is occurring in every moment. We don't always see it but when we work with the method we become aware of it. In doing so, we know that no-one can ever do anything "wrong" and that every act is a loving act. Every event is an equilibrating event, and all events are part of the divine order of the Universe. They are an expression to bring any imbalance back into balance and into the centre which is love... pure love. I have experienced various forms of this love, from white light to heartfelt gratitude and overwhelming feeling of love for everyone to warmth and a glow as I understood the love surrounding me.

I experienced all of the above from working the scientific method with wonderful facilitators trained by Dr J F Demartini, and by applying the method myself. I am now purposeful in how I look at life and its events, I make an effort to be as present as possible so I can maximise on the magnificent life experience that has been given to me and to you—it's around you right now.

Mental—Awaken Your Genius

Would you love to be clear in your thoughts, to be logical, rational and have the ability to choose thoughts that serve you? Mentally we only use a fraction of our brain. Each thought builds a neural pathway in the brain and if exercised the thoughts become faster and more agile. By making more connections we can learn to build more neural pathways in our brain and develop the ability to rapidly see opportunities as they arise, because we have made the connection.

I have increased my mental abilities to study and retain information about areas of life in which I am interested. After my first weekend at The Breakthrough Experience®, I went through a "quickening" which led me to reading book after book from Brisbane City Library. By "quickening" I mean that the inspiration which comes from God was guiding me to find further information so I could follow through on my mission.) Interestingly the right book would appear to pop out of the shelf, beckoning me to read it.

No sooner than I had read a book, I would be offered the next progression for my spiritual journey.

Notable authors for me were Dr Wayne Dyer, Louise Hay, and Eckhart Tolle. This is not to forget Deepak Chopra or of course, the works of Dr J F Demartini. On my long trips into the city I used to play audio tapes of John's and also listen to Deepak and Wayne. Again, similar to the books it always seemed to me that I would receive the right message at the right time for whatever I was doing.

Attending The Prophecy Experience™ with Global 1 Training—Dr J F Demartini's seven day inspirational and mind-expanding course—also stretched my mind well beyond its usual range of thought which is both healthy and life enriching. The more you learn the more inspired you become to learn more and this enables you to integrate your new leanings and find greater equilibrium for your life. Would I go back to being tired and uninspired? No way Jose!

Vocational—Your Purpose In Life

The critical key to making your work feel like a holiday is to do what you love and love what you do. Can you say that about your career and job role? If you can't then you will benefit from exploring what it is that you would love to do. Often people are hemmed in by others values of what they believe they should be doing. Do you notice your inner voice? Is it wanting you to break fee? Are you unhappy at your work? Is it a struggle? Are you happy in your work but you would like to serve greater numbers of clients? Do you want actualise your dreams? Or do you want improve the effectiveness and efficiency within your business?

These all seem like simple questions and of course there are pragmatic steps that you can take towards finding the answers. The Demartini Method is the only method I know that breaks through the underlying psychology of whatever it is that may be holding you back. When you learn to write down your true and inspiring goals, you will realize that they are not exaggerated or minimised objectives—they are set in realistic and accurate timeframes. They become fixed when both your heart and your mind are aligned. These are the goals that will accomplish the greatest achievements.

It has been interesting for me, as I have always loved what I do for a career, however I have often not been appreciated, which I am thankful for because along the way I have been guided towards my true mission. Since I did The Demartini Method® and set my goals out, I needed to maintain my usual role in order to provide for myself and my daughter and pay the mortgage, and so my own transition to my dream career has been a selective and carefully-stepped approach.

Financial—Creating Your Fortune

You can learn how to appreciate the value of money, how to build self-worth and manage more money and resources. You can learn how to earn money doing what you love. Gain the confidence to play a bigger game as you begin to invest wisely and send out the messages to the Universe that your inner and outer worth are valuable. Results are about you and your journey, about what you want to achieve. Don't be fooled with "Get rich quick" schemes. Emotions and money do not mix well and so quick gains can become quick losses. Dr J F Demartini's teachings and logical approaches to wealth-building allow you to be balanced, focussed and ready to make wise decisions in terms of your actions.

I worked with Rowan Burn on his Purpose Power Wealth program regularly attending his webinar's. It was at one of these webinars that Rowan threw out a challenge to everyone. It was a prize of some consultancy for the first person to come up with a thousand benefits of having financial wealth! Now this is an example of inspiration and what can happen when you get on mission. I returned a list to him within 24 hours; I wanted the prize because I wanted to work on my loss. I knew it would lead me to success in unravelling the loss. After that, I initially set targets and goals to become more independent and to be able to fund my love of The Demartini Method®. I wanted to have enough money to afford being able to take my family on good holidays and to be able to treat them and make their lives more comfortable. I planned to be valued more for my work and efforts and for this to translate into more income. To date I have been able to attend every event of The Breakthrough Experience® in Australia and to attend The Demartini Method® Training Program each year. I have been able to negotiate around my work situations and to have that freedom to attend these seminars—something I never ever felt I was empowered to do in the past.

Whilst I have had the Universe turn me upside down and test me on my strength of belief, the journey sees me land back on my feet every single time, no matter what challenge or adversity I have come to face. The Universe guides people who follow their mission and calling in life. The point I want to make is not that you can achieve what I have, which may not fit with your circumstances and mission, but that you have the power and control in your own hands to set out and achieve what you want to in your own life. The method will see you improve on your current situation and set you on a trajectory that will see you transform your wealth into what you want it to be.

Family—Your Sense of Belonging

It is amazing how many people go through life not truly connecting with their family members. Our closest relationships can be the dearest. They are designed to reveal the character traits which we are not owning or appreciating within ourselves. Very often when we really dislike a trait or we label a family member, then it is ourselves that we are hurting the most. Judgments, if left too long, can lead to illness in the physical body. Using The Demartini Method®, you can manage family conflicts and deep rooted judgements and allow the pathways of communication to open up. When we understand each other's values, and we can communicate according to those values then we achieve the results we are looking for. How would you like to resolve a long standing conflict? Would you like to improve communication with a family member? Would you like to share more love and intimacy?

I dreamt of being able to embrace my own parents and value them more. I desired to appreciate their values and be able to communicate according to their values and not in mine. I have been able to see how they have and are subconsciously helping me with my mission, and how they are also consciously doing that. I could not see it before I practiced The Demartini Method®. I see it now and it blows me away, as I so appreciate their love.

I spend more quality time with my daughter and family. We have had some inspiring and rewarding holidays together and I am certain that my appreciation of them has led to me being able to see the love and gratitude in them. Perfect!

Social—Your Level of Influence

Do you want to increase your personal and social power within your community? Do you want to build and nurture your networks and associations? Do you want to initiate a social transformation of any kind? Working The Demartini Method® can open up your sphere of influence and bring opportunities knocking on your door. How far you go depends on what you are wanting and are willing to do. I can guarantee that however stuck you may be feeling, I can open up the inspiration which will start the ball rolling in the direction that you want.

Once I had seen a vision for my mission, I set myself a six month plan, listing the finer details of what I needed to do to achieve my outcomes. I wanted to take careful steps initially and find my feet. Pursuing my dreams whilst maintaining an income in a lower priority line of work is definitely a challenge but it is not impossible. My first step of writing a book has led to me meeting all kinds of people who have helped me with my purpose. These have ranged from opportunities to meet up and explore a great network which invariably attracts clients wanting and needing the method. I have met people from all walks of life. What can I say? I have met literally hundreds of wonderful people! I started to go to meet-ups around Brisbane and listen to others presenting, or sharing their stories. I have met other Authors. Again this is incredible for me and I feel a tear of gratitude because if you only knew how tired and worn out I was, you would appreciate the dramatic transformation that Dr J F Demartini's method brought to me. There is no way I could have worked all day and then gone to a meet-up. Where my life felt closed off as a single parent, a window of opportunity was opening up and this was inspiring. Some of the people I have met have given me jewels of information for which I am grateful. I have been able to learn many useful presentation skills, selling techniques, latest website tricks and social media. I have also met Wayne Dyer, Cheryl Richardson and Reid from Hay House. Yes, meeting Wayne was one of my ambitions! I have also met people with the most heart inspiring stories that feed my inspiration further.

Physical—Your Vitality in Life

If you want to enhance your wellbeing and nutrition or improve exercise regimes, build endurance and stamina or maintain your attractiveness and beauty, then The Demartini Method® can work for you. There are Demartini Method® facilitators in Australia and around the world who are working with top sportsmen and women improving their skills and getting great results. As it was for me I needed to maintain and increase my vital energy as I had definitely lost my spark before finding John.

I went from an inability to find the energy to getting up and walking the dog for half an hour before going to work. I have begun regular long walks and improved my dog's life and my own enjoyment of the outdoors. I rise at 5.00 am and exercise in the park as I take the dog on her walk. It is often dark and I now mediate and practice my gratitude which always has beautiful knock on effects. I began yoga classes, and I was even able to take my daughter along too. The yoga is so wonderful. I was also able to pay for weekly chiropractic sessions which aligned my brain to my spine. The chiropractor was cognisant of the work of Dr. J F Demartini and we shared many great conversations over my mission, the power of chiropractic work and the health of people today. I am grateful to him he not only had a genuine commitment to supporting his clients, but emanated a wonderful energy that was uplifting and gave me the support I needed during my transformation.

Having begun more sporting activities to improve my physical health I notice that I receive more compliments about my looks and others have noticed that I am more toned. In fact it's funny that they think I have lost weight, but I know that I haven't. Mastering The Seven Areas of Your Life

Indeed, by mastering the seven areas you can actually become the creator and innovator of your own destiny. You become the artist that can paint your own landscape or you become the director of your own symphony and instead of fearing life you begin to let go and start moving in synchronicity with the dance of life. Beginning the dance is easy: all you need to do is take the first step and start the movement.

CHAPTER 13

The True Light Of Loss

"We can easily forgive a child who is afraid of the dark; the real tragedy of life is when we men are afraid of the light."

Plato, Greek Author & Philosopher in Athens
(427–347 BC)

The headline quote infers that it is a tragedy of life if men are afraid of the light. This book has been my way to show you my insights into the power of transformation and how loss, when understood, is a strong and life enriching experience that open the doors for you to not only see the beauty that life offers you, but to enable you to be enriched with the gains that experiencing loss can bring. There are many amazing principles in The Breakthrough Experience® with Dr J F Demartini. I would like to share the following principles to start you on your journey of transformation:

Principle 7: "Your ideas and thoughts, when unsteadied by emotions, will undergo periodic emotional cycles-revolutions. Anything you don't love you will re-peat or "pre-peat" until you love it."

And **Principle 31:** "Your ideas and thoughts can stretch and shrink the truth and distort the fabric of space-time."

"The truth is what it is, as it is. What is, as it is, is Love.

The will of God is love. The will of God is equilibrium.

When the gains don't equal the losses, you lie."

At the time of my sisters deaths, my ideas and thoughts stretched the truth—as I perceived a loss. This in fact was a big, emotional lie that I was telling myself. In doing this, I unknowingly and unconsciously set myself up to undergo periodic emotional cycles and revolutions throughout my life. Well, yes in truth I had 'lost' my twin sisters, but the laws of the Universe require a full quantum of energy in order for us to evolve through life. This means that everything is always in equilibrium. So, the lie I was telling myself is that there were no gains and that I had only experienced loss. In my perception, there was no blessing inside my emotional trauma as a child. The truth is that any grief I was experiencing at the time was in fact to counterbalance the infatuation or addictions to certain traits in my sisters, and to awaken the imbalance to the relief of their deaths that I was choosing not to recognise in my mind.

When light is shone onto what these traits are and The Demartini Method® for Loss is applied, I am able to see how the traits were being balanced out and by whom, and what the benefits and drawbacks were to the imbalance of lies that I was telling myself. By undergoing the balancing exercise in my mind, I can in fact dissolve any remaining grief and dissolve any lies that I may be telling myself. In doing this I am freeing myself from the repetitive and periodic lifecycle that has been pervading my life. And so can you. I must say for the purposes of keeping this simple in order for you to understand the process, that I will select one trait in my sisters that I was infatuated with. The trait was in the games we played together. I perceived my sisters to be 'fun'. Now, remember that any trait which you are infatuated with and which is then withdrawn you will create a withdrawal symptom— that withdrawal symptom is called grief. No trait is ever missing, and if we look closely enough in our lives we will see that it has just changed form. No person or their traits ever really disappears, it is only in our perception that they do. As Dr J F Demartini quotes, "The master lives in a world of transformation, the masses live in the illusion of gain and loss."

In the example I have given, I asked myself the following question: Who was providing me with the same enjoyment with respect to playing games? As I answered it, I saw that my neighbourhood friends, my primary school friends, and (at Christmas time) it was my mum and dad and their friend's children. We had a lot of fun at Christmas time and I cherished the times we shared, which certainly helped to remove the grief. With all of these new friends, I shared the same sort of "secret seven" games— playing in the woods, dancing and making things. The benefit of the new form of game playing was that I travelled further afield and played with more than just my two sisters. I got to experience what it was like having brothers. I learnt more types of games, and I got to be more physical. I also got the opportunity to share my fun with other people outside of the family. We shared our toys and belongings, we designed new things together, and we went on adventures. As I looked at the drawbacks of playing games and having fun with the twins, I saw that it was restrictive and it kept me totally within the family—insular in a way. It also included all the arguments that I had had with them as a sister. Sometimes when the games turned sour, we would fall out and not speak to each other. Sometimes things went wrong and I got blamed because I was the youngest. This would easily lead to me having to bear the punishment when I wasn't solely to blame. This would make me cross with them and hate them for it. For some reason my mind, at the point of their death and after, chooses to block out these feelings and emotions.

Once I look at other perceptions rather than totally focussing on the infatuated trait that I have lost, I can see that losing it in the form it was, opened my life up to new influences and wider choices and options. I can also see that the old form had a set of drawbacks to it which I had chosen to ignore and didn't miss because, in fact, one can only experience relief over release from traits that are resented. Can you see that?

I can now fully appreciate the loss of that trait and how it changed form after their deaths. Having done that with all traits of infatuation the grief subsides. By looking at the benefits of the new form and the drawbacks of the old form we can balance the perception and centre the emotions. When this is done for all traits we experience the truth and the truth is that love is all there is.

It is only now, after 40 years, that I am at last balancing the emotion of loss of my twin sisters. As I mentioned earlier the imbalanced emotions set up a pattern and a cycle of repetition because as **Principle 7** expresses, "Anything you don't love you will re-peat or "pre-peat" until you love it."

Whilst in my autobiography there are many perceived imbalances, what I want to do for the purpose of this book is to keep it as simple as I can. I want to show you the repeated cycles, and how, each time, the Universe will give you a stronger wakeup call than before, until it finally reaches a peak and you decide you can no longer bear any more perceptions or feelings of pain so you take steps towards changing what can be changed.

The purpose of my book—my story, my life—is to show you these things so that you know that you do not have to go through from any unwanted emotions that for long periods of time are running your life and interfering with your mission. You can nip it in the bud early on in your life instead of letting it weigh you down for years to come—and then you can live a fulfilled and inspiring life. I am not saying here that you will never experience a loss because that is unrealistic. What I am saying is that you can change the form and you can balance the emotions so that the Universe won't send you a stronger message.

The diagram overleaf shows my waves of emotion about loss increasing over time from the age of nine until today. The top part of the diagram represents the infatuations which cause the grief when a loss arises. For my sisters, I had a certain infatuation that triggered me to experience the emotions of grief. My mind, as I described earlier, was ignoring the 'relief elements'—the relief inside of me that my sisters had passed away. Like Dr J F Demartini also teaches, when we 'lose' resentment, it's a gain in our perception—because we're 'happy' when something we resent disappears from our lives. Another quote from Dr J F Demartini that explains this neatly is, "The greater the grief, the greater the relief."

The diagram represents how losing the twins and placing myself in the position of burying the grief, and hiding the relief was not learning to love the loss. The following are the key emotional charges around my hidden loss and a description of how they attracted further scenarios to happen in my life as they attempted to wake me up to the truth.

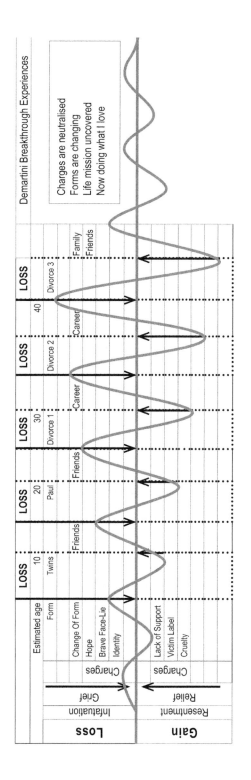

Demartini Breakthrough Experiences

Charges are neutralised
Forms are changing
Life mission uncovered
Now doing what I love

Infatuations

Hoping Beyond Hope

You might remember back in *Chapter 1* that I was wishing on the chicken bone for the impossible to happen; it was what kept me going. It was an infatuation and because it was an imbalance and an unrealistic expectation on life, the Universe sent more despairing scenarios for me to handle. After all, hoping beyond hope was the message I was giving out to everyone around me.

Brave Face

By putting on a brave face, I was in fact wearing a mask. Behind the mask the grief was hidden. Again, this is like telling the Universe I want more situations like this. So as a mirror, I married people who showed me blatantly that I was lieing. In going through these marriages I would consistently put my brave face on again at work, in front of people. Inside the pain of what I was feeling was hurt, and so to counter-balance the pain I would need to numb the pain with tobacco and alcohol. That requires a lot of drinking and cigarettes I can tell you!

Resentments

Lack Of Support During Grief

The resentment of perceiving a lack of support at the time of the twins' death drove my addiction to support from my parents and friends, leading to me never quite feeling like I could stand up on my own two feet. I lacked confidence. This had a further flow-on effect as I travelled through my career, preferring to always step back and let a more confident person through, even if I knew inwardly that I could handle the situation. Again, the energy I sent out to the Universe would be telling it to recreate the situation where I could then feel unsupported in order to come to an appreciation of it.

Cruelty—Being Labelled As A Victim

Do you recall in *Chapter 2* how David Straw taunted me over the death of my sisters? Do you remember how this pushed a button inside me, and how my family would just watch me cry, and not even ask me how I was? I realise now that the cruelty was trying to get me to cry and release some of my pent up emotions—perhaps even help other caregivers to see that I was struggling. Now, because I continued to resent that cruelty and not love it, **Principle** 7 kicked in and through each marriage I was attracted an increase in physically tense situations as each incident was the Universes' attempt to awaken my life.

My "Lost & Alone" Identity

I resented losing my identity of being a "triplet" and associated with the twins. Mum had always dressed us to look the same and so I felt the loss of that when they died. It was like part of me died with them and the other part was so alone. This resentment was to cause me numerous attempted wakeups in a bid to counter the balance. My lost and alone identity was building up as more and more situations that cause feelings of low self-worth were occurring. As I ignored them, they built up to alarming proportions, involving the police and courts, to wake me up to my own identity.

Finally, I believe it took Stuart to alert me to the invasion on my identity for me to finally wake up to the imbalance that had been happening. What a relief it is to finally say hello to Lynn Hope Thomas and goodbye to repeated loneliness. I am grateful to each of my relationships for bringing me on that path of discovery and enlightenment.

Points to Help You

Whatever you are dealing with in terms of loss, the reasons for the grief will be similar in that you are focussed on the traits that you admire and so feel the grief. You may have been in some very difficult circumstances and it can be really hard to find the benefits in those situations. The benefits are there, I assure you, whatever your situation is.

In my pursuit and ongoing evolution as a professionally-trained Demartini Method® facilitator, I have attended many meetings in which

I have witnessed extreme events and have been able to guide people through these to a place of gratitude and love. I have witnessed other facilitators and John do the same so I know with absolute certainty and presence that any event can be resolved and of course I know my own circumstances which have been difficult at times.

As a final note I will share with you some of actions and activities that I have undertaken along the way, and some of the things I now do which I consider to be supportive of a healthy lifestyle in terms of all the main areas of life; being the physical, mental, family, social, financial, spiritual and vocational aspects.

Listen to your heart or your inner voice, and trust your intuition. Sometimes our life gets so busy we allow it to drown out our spiritual voices. Try taking up Yoga this is a great way to reconnect the mind, body and spirit. If that is too hard for you, and I hope it isn't, then try breathing exercises. Breathing deeply and reconnecting with your breath can relieve a lot of stress as can physical exercise. Now, when it comes to exercise, there is nothing easier than walking! You put one foot in front of the other and off you go! It's as easy as anything. Recall that I went from finding it too hard to take the dog for a walk to now exercising regularly, the dog loves it and I feel so much more energised and whilst walking it gives me time to meditate, breathe and focus on my mission and gratitude. Yes, being grateful to God for whatever is happening in our lives is not only liberating, it sends the right messages and energy out to the Universe so that you eventually begin to see remarkable and interesting things coming back to you. If you don't believe it, try it—you have nothing to lose.

Researching on the Internet is time consuming however, it can lead to a whole lot of inspiration and support. Try looking for support groups, make connections with people, chat across the ether, you are safe and you might just learn a thing or two that can really help you. As you pass through each day there will be ups and downs and people who push your buttons. Treat everyone as yourself, remember they are working to the best of their ability, however limited and ignorant it may be. You can chose your reactions and learn to become a master of change and transformation. It is a very liberating feeling. Letting go is sometimes a difficult thing but allow yourself to pass through change and you will see that most of the reactions related to fears and often the fears themselves are not half as real as we imagine them to be. I hope you can now see how grateful I am to Daniela Stalling who introduced to me Dr J F Demartini. This one act of friendship, trust and certainty opened up the means for me to re-evaluate my life events, and put me consciously on mission. It has seen me go from tired to inspired and write a book to deliver an inspirational message to those people who want and need to understand their losses.

I am so appreciative of John and how he has tirelessly devoted his life to understanding human behaviour and then for sharing his learning's with us. Not only does he do that week in and week out, he does it with love and certainty. I now begin to see very clearly that God really does work in mysterious ways. I intend to continue sharing my own love, certainty and inspiration with people and that means writing more books that show people examples of how The Demartini Method® can transform their lives. My mission is to bring back smiles to the faces that have once had tears of sadness on them through their misperceptions. If that means revealing a part of me to you, then that is a small sacrifice to pay because I know that the ripple effect of my work will multiply. I love working to solve problems, I love analysing scenarios. No matter how complicated you perceive your loss to be, or whatever other dynamics you perceive to be involved, you can be assured that just as I have applied myself to break through my own complicated loss, I will do the same for you. I open my heart to you, and I hold out my hand for those individuals needing to break through loss.

What Is Hope?

By Lynn Hope Thomas

It is the light that carried you through the darkest of days.
A faint and whispering thread of a possible connection that will keep you alive
For each and every moment that talks you into dying…
Another whisper called hope will talk you into living.
For each and every time that you have felt like giving up and dying.
There will always be a reason for living.
And somehow the same that carried you through birth in the first instance,
Will also carry you through each and every moment.
Why?
Because you are worth it!
God is omnipresent and loves you!
Because you have inside of you a purpose and
A dream that needs to unfold, and
It needs to live longer than a day!
Can you honestly let a thought dampen your dream?
Can you honestly let a thought extinguish your flame?
No matter what your body,
No matter what your now,
Never, not ever, give up on that thread of light.
It is your saviour,
Be it your light, be it your Master, be it your child, your partner, your love
Simply know that flicker of hope as LOVE.
Hope is in my heart,
Hope you understand,
Hope you learn, and
Hope you teach to others
Love IS.

APPENDIX

The Appendix consists of notes, lessons and learning's that I experienced on my journey as I wrote Breaking Through Loss. The idea of sharing these personal moments is to give insight into what happens when you embark on a transformation. I've also chosen to connect with other leading people who have written inspiring quotes as these messages often provide honey along the path.

Wisdom and Balance

"Wisdom is maximal when you acknowledge the existing balance and order in yourself and others."

Dr. John Demartini

22nd November, 2010

My contract ended on Friday after having spent a wonderful week on Dr. John Demartini's Prophecy 1 Experience ™. It was the perfect balance to keep me centred and boy does a one-sided awareness feel awful. I left the City Council on Friday without even a word from any manager. It had been my agent who rang me earlier in the week to give me the news. Another council employee apologised to me for the lack of respect shown; for all the policies on how to treat people I was simply a nobody, but in being so, I was everything, somehow it was another sign of being on the right path.

The previous Thursday, John had tasked us with a simple but wonderful meditation exercise where we allowed ourselves to be attracted to aspects of nature in the park. We selected five things and then wrote how they represented a significant message to us. For me, the bright yellow flower represented the sun which was telling me to trust in God's plan. Well today I appear to have forgotten that! I am feeling anxious and frightened, I have so many things to do, I am feeling guilty that each thing is the wrong thing and I'm going to suffer devastating consequences. Yuk!! I want to let out an almighty scream…God why do you always…Stop! God how grateful I am that you are always sending me loving signs of where I need to put my efforts and direction. Great! I've just had a burst of tears, realised that I can be kinder to myself, after all as a single mother with no income, feeling a bit crap is okay isn't it? Then I suddenly remember Marie who lost her father three weeks ago, and now I am feeling determined that I will get myself out of this mire, the beauty of which is in the actual pain and suffering, though it feels so horrid.

Synchronicity

"With Synchronicity, all the resources we need are made available to us at the precise moment that is appropriate. The people who come into our lives are the ones we need at that moment in time. Everything is perfect. We only need to recognise this to tune into the flow. Everything happens for a Reason and Every Experience is a Learning Experience."

Alex Chua

23rd November, 2010

I wanted to share a little synchronicity with you. The concept was developed by Carl Jung and his personal experiences that seemed to indicate there was more to coincidences than we realise.

Carl Jung said: *"The universal principle is found even in the smallest particle, which therefore corresponds to the whole."* Synchronicity, An Acausal Connecting Principle, by C G Jung.

Below are the words from an e-mail where my friend sees the synchronicity in my communication to her:

"This is so freaky I just sent you an email at the same time I received yours!"

In recent weeks I have been to a couple of libraries and found that by "coincidence" I am led to the books that I want and need to read. It is absolutely synchronous that I find the appropriate book for the stage I am at in my understanding and comprehension.

Have faith and confidence that the Universe will lead you to the right things you need for your growth!

Reminder of a life lost

In most cases, suicide is a solitary event and yet it has often far-reaching repercussions for many others.

It is rather like throwing a stone into a pond; the ripples spread and spread.

ALISON WERTHEIMER, A Special Scar

25th November, 2010

I'm working on chapter three today. I need to lose some weight so that I can fit into the bridesmaids dress for my friend's wedding next month. To do this, after dropping my daughter at pre-school care at 6.30am I go to the local swimming baths and swim for an hour. It's Chapter 3 and Day 3 of the diet. I'm hungry.

This morning there was a memorial service for Valerie Moreton who died, whilst suffering from depression., leaving behind her beautiful family and also a nine year old daughter. I was just starting to get to know Valerie, a lovely smiling girl, always had time to talk, not like some. Boy did it strike me hard! In fact her death was a signal to me to make sure that I changed my path that I had to make some sense of these deaths and heartbreak. I wanted to help people like her daughter who was now suffering a grief and that's why I am writing this book, it's to support those who at some point in their lives might come across grief and loss, and then need to find a way through it. I want to highlight the harm it can do if not fully understood and worked through.

I want to show that there is a terrific method out there to help and assist you overcomes it, in a faster and healthier way.

Writing a Book

*"My aim is to put down on paper what I see and
what I feel in the best and simplest way."*

Ernest Hemingway

26ᵗʰ November, 2010

What a great day! I assisted the Global 1 team in the New Wave conference in Brisbane. It was an absolute delight; I got to hang out with these really young and cool people from Sydney, Russia, and the UK. It was great working with inspired people.

And not only that, I could see my mentors Dale Beaumont, Rowan Burn and Dr John Demartini.

Dale Beaumont is the person who has sown the seed to write a book, he was so genuine and convincing after his free one day talk that I signed up for. On the course I was amazed: this guy knows his stuff, but not only that he gives, gives and gives. The guy is a legend at what he does. A beautiful person, determined and driven with ambition. Thank you Dale.

Be Your Authentic Self

*"Your authentic self is who you are when you have no
fear of judgment or before the world starts pushing
you around and telling you who you're supposed to
be. Your fictional self is who you are when you have a
social mask on to please everyone else. Give yourself
permission to be your authentic self."*

Dr. Phil

Rowan remarked on my blue eyes, the same ones looking at him and seeing in his eyes the same spark that will drive us forward. This is what John talks about, this is what John teaches, authenticity. To communicate with another person who is being authentic is absolutely loving and therapeutic.

Whilst Writing Chapter 3

"Your life does not get better by chance,
it gets better by change."

Jim Rohn

1ˢᵗ December, 2010

I spent a lovely time in Church listening to the Year 4 children present the assembly. It warmed my heart to witness the spirit of God within them as they were singing joyfully. I really am seeing more beauty each day, and I am thankful. This spurred me on to a planned meeting with an agent to find work. It's my second week of no income, and I am fortunate to have taken heed to maintain a degree of liquidity, thanks to Dr. John Demartini.

What a lovely girl the agent was, we talked and talked so fluidly. She picked up my vibes for certain, and complimented me on my dedication to my job. I was even able to explain to her that I also had a new tool in my kit bag and that it would enable me to overcome any difficulties on projects. I could not tell her enough about Dr. John Demartini's work. She listened and absorbed everything and I saw in her eyes and face what my true work will be and must be with The Demartini Method®. Working The Demartini Method® and inspiring others to follow their mission, and if not their mission then inspiring them in their workplaces, being part of a change in corporate cultures. Thank you, Linda, for meeting me that day, it was a great pleasure. In keeping with my desire to progress on my life journey in a healthier manner, I worked The Demartini Method® today on the benefits and drawbacks of marriage and also the benefits and drawbacks of being single. I can now see why it was imperative that my marriages ended and I can see my personal growth has been at the maximum whilst being on my own. You don't need the security of a man's income to get you through; in fact you can live a fulfilled life and experience the beauty of overcoming challenges without it.

The thing about perceived emotional pain is that you have to feel it if it's going to do any good. You also have to love it for what it is.

Feelings Outpour Like A River

"Heaven knows we need never be ashamed of our tears, for they are rain upon the blinding dust of earth, overlying our hard hearts"

Charles Dickens, Great Expectations, 1860

3rd December, 2010

Last night I was re-writing Chapter 3; I didn't finish, I became consumed with emotion. This morning I feel very low, these feelings have to come out. They are the part of me that has been suppressed for many years. I don't like the feelings, I want to cry. Hmm, do I want to cry a river? Feels like it, do I want to cry like Niagara Falls? No, it's not that bad and then I smile. By keeping centred I can limit the extremes of these emotions.

I can trust myself to handle what God had given me, what my sisters gave me. Dr. John Demartini says, "I don't want to hear your story, so work the method." I want to and will, but at times identifying the charges is difficult. By writing my story I can find the charges.

Well done Jodie Baxter, and thank you for sharing with me how you worked the method during a very difficult time during your father's illness and subsequent passing. It is wholesome to hear that it helped you. That's what I have to do. I have to work every charge I had during that period of time and dissolve it, then I can move forward. Writing this book will help me to identify where there is a charge and then I can dissolve it.

Student at Work

"When the student is ready, the master appears."

Buddhist Proverb

5th December, 2010

Today I knew I needed to spend time on basic household duties. It's alright for the wealthy to talk about only spending time on high value work and paying someone else for low value work. The reality is that when you have no money, it's completely hard, without swearing, to get to that point!

Yet let me be quite clear, those who have gone from nothing to being rich, have managed to fight through the pain of it. So learn a lesson here as quickly as you can.

I have to suffer this period but I will be persistent and continue down the same path no matter how hard it seems. For me, the next arduous task was the gardening! The lawn needed mowing, I'm a girl I don't do lawns! Don't fight it Lynn! Let go!

I knew the bin was wretched! I had to do something about the bin. There are maggots in there! Having a nine year old means the bin frequently gets half eaten stuff, not tightly wrapped, and with the heat and all, it soon breeds the perfect environment for maggots. I was more than hopeful because on Friday the bin men just simply take it all away! Or so I hoped. Not this time, there was a slim plastic wrapper, a "see through" wrapper, and all I could see were maggots! Hundreds and hundreds stuck to the bottom of the bin. I wanted to be so in control and sorted, that I attempted to get rid of them. This was awesomely brave of me; I shudder at the thought of maggots. Typical girly, I can scream and jump and do the flamenco! I started slowly spraying the top of the bin with water, yuk! I progressed to flipping the lid and spraying the top in cycles down, I then decided to tip the bin, which kind of ended up strewn across the road! The gun fell off the hose and water spurted everywhere! I then had to jump across the line of white worms and straight to the phone…Dad! Help me!

The amused look on his face said it all when he saw the bin in the middle of the road and me in tatters! He then proceeded to teach me, "Look Lynn its simple, flies lay eggs on meat, maggots emerge, then they form a crystal, then they emerge as flies, that's the cycle." There is nothing to fear!" And in his teaching I was aware of the truth, the infinite wisdom in all of creation takes us through the cycle of birth, and then death and then where?

I know that at his latter age, Dad wants to teach me everything he knows, how great is his love for me. I truly appreciate what he says. My dad, I love him.

Disappointment Wanes

*"I don't want my fans to have the same
disappointment as me when I was refused by some
players to sign my notebook when I was young."*

Ronaldo, Brazilian Soccer Player

13" December, 2010

I was excited I had an interview. It started off really well, I was confident and answered the questions well. Mmm, seemed to go a bit stale towards the end. While I answered the question, it would appear that she did not understand my answer.

I always start off hopefully, I prepare well, I put a lot into it and then yep, it's not to be. The feedback was awful. To be told that you are nervous and lacked experience is "bizarre" to say the least. Perhaps what she saw in me was a mirrored reflection of her.

The comments were almost the opposite of what I felt had happened. I can't help it, sometimes it's hard to shrug off the feeling. Maybe I prepare too well, am too hopeful, too positive and so the Universe knocks me back or maybe the Universe is keen for me to finish my book.

Frustration Leads To Inspiration

Thanks To Friends

14th December, 2010

Today I am somewhat subdued. I can't seem to let go of wanting to hear about the job role. I'm reading some Deepak Chopra and trying to take advice here. I am aware that I am not helping my situation by worrying; I feel it in the pit of my stomach. Today I have two young children to look after and being able to get to my pc and continue writing my story is difficult.

I finally got onto Facebook and read a message posted by Stella Sherone, it basically said, 'When the day has you feeling emotional, get on with production.'—I was so grateful to Stella as that piece of advice absolutely spoke to me. Then fellow facilitator Karla Mayas, a friend from Hungary, was telling me what an inspirational lady I was, and how she wanted to work with me. I am humbled. I feel a tear there that someone recognises what I am trying to achieve and that I can inspire others. I am inspirational, I am working towards my highest value, I have been inspired ever since I met Dr. John Demartini and nothing will stop me getting my book written and published and sold around the world. Then I can start to give my own inspirational talks and begin the much needed work of helping people who may be suffering.

Double Rainbows at Mooloolaba

"If you want the rainbow,
you've got to put up with the rain."
Dolly Parton

17th December, 2010

Wow, I set off for a friend's wedding in Mooloolaba. I travelled with another friend who first introduced me to Dr J F Demartini, yet ever since I embarked on my path, our friendship has drifted into her not really connecting with me anymore. By this, I mean I make attempts to talk to her, but it's clear I am not high on her list of values. I've learnt to let go, I was sad at first but new friends are coming into my life, and this is always the case. I took the opportunity to share the ride. I am beginning to learn patience, and to keep my thoughts open and look for the benefits.

A truly remarkable incident occurred after a long walk on the beach in the evening. The thunderstorms were approaching and soon there was a lot of drizzly rain and it went very dark. We sat on the balcony watching the rain and all of a sudden we were enveloped in light, really bright light. I recall saying, "Hey, we're in the light!" It felt warm and beautiful. Then over the ocean, one and then two rainbows appeared, full circle, bright colours. I did my best to capture the beauty on my camera, but for some reason the camera couldn't get the light. It was so fluorescent, more than I have ever seen. The rainbows were so present I felt great appreciation for God. Needless to say, the wedding the next day was beautiful, it was perfect, full of love. As I searched for a quote on the Internet to head up this diary moment I came across a YouTube clip of a double rainbow by Hungrybear. It kind of sums up how great I felt at seeing the double rainbow and being

111

bathed in its light. You must listen to it, it's very funny and has had 34 million views and been liked by over 200,000 people— awesome!

http://www.youtube.com/watch?v=OQSNhk5ICTI

Gratitude, Gratitude

*To put the world in order, we must first put the
nation in order; to put the nation in order, we must
put the family in order; to put the family in order, we
must cultivate our personal life; and to cultivate our
personal life, we must first set our hearts right.*
Confucius (BC 551–BC 479), Chinese philosopher

22nd December, 2010

I went to see Santa about what my daughter would be getting for Christmas. Not having worked for over four weeks is kind of rife for negative thoughts and battling them is my new form of mental fitness. You know the EGO is so cocky, it wants to blame everyone around me for this predicament; it does not want to understand that this is truly transformational. I am moving out of an egotistic state into a relationship with God, where I can now fly like a bird and not worry about where my next feed will come from.

Love is sustaining me, love is the wind beneath my wings, love is my family, love is the knock backs, love is the disappointments, and love is everything and everyone. Embracing all this love with open arms is the key to sustaining balance. Love thy enemy. Of course only now do I truly understand.

Thank you for today. Today was a gift and I have worked hard to open my eyes and see for the first time the beauty all around me. Thank you to myself, I love you Lynn Hope Thomas and I am so, so grateful that you are taking this journey. Keep following your dreams and triumph every hurdle!

More Gratitude's!

23rd December, 2010

1. Thank you for the interview today and the practice of responding to difficult questioning. If I don't succeed, then I will be prepared for the next interview and it's only a matter of time. Thank you to my neighbour who allows my dog to play with his puppy Hugo, we had a lovely chat and he is so neighbourly, I hope he enjoys his vacation to the US/ Canada.

2. Thank you to my lovely friend Julia and Karla Mayas, any worries floated away upon talking to you.

3. Thank you to my Facebook friends who open my heart with all the wonderful information that they share.

4. Thanks to Mum & Dad, Dad for being so healthy this week and not needing any heart surgery, Mum for looking after Lauren and her friend at the ice rink, while I went for the interview.

5. Thank you Michelle for always making Mum's hair look so good and for being a reliable friend.

6. Thank you to my other friends who are there and not there when I feel I need you.

7. Thank you to the weather for being so interesting and changeable, I love the cloud formations.

8. Thank you for it being Christmas and the special little things that go with it like buying solar lights as cheaply as $3 at Kmart, thanks Kmart.

9. Thank you for all the Masters and Authors for writing great books for me to read and learn from.

10. Thank you to myself for working hard and being diligent to save, thank you to my mentor, Rowan, for his kind words and encouragement.

11. Thank you God and the Universe for this wonderful opportunity called life, and for allowing me to live and enjoy the splendour of every breath.

12. Thank you to my Yoga teacher, Lisa, for teaching me to breathe and relax and de-stress and learn how my body can be at one with the Universe.

13. Thank you for all the rain, I don't need to water my garden and my grass is still alive.

14. Thank you Dad for putting up my new patio decorations and the new wipe board.

15. Thank you Lynn for all your hard work and your beautiful home.

16. Thank you Universe for allowing me this spare time to write my book.

17. Thank you for allowing me the time to live life at a pace of my own choosing rather than at an employer's pace.

18. Thank you Dr. John Demartini.

19. Thank you to my friend who introduced me to Dr J F Demartini.

20. Thank you to my friend's mother who introduced her to Dr J F Demartini.

21. Thank you to those Facebook friends who help me to understand myself better and mirror disowned aspects which I need to work on.

22. Thank you for the list of traits that I can work on and love myself more.

23. Thank you to my neighbours for all being there.

24. Thank you to the out of school care who give Lauren heaps and heaps of love.

25. Thank you to the school and the teachers, they are truly amazing.

26. Thank you for all contrasts in the world, for helping us to see the upside and underside of life.

27. Thank you for my life here in Australia.

28. Thank you for allowing me to be in your country.

29. Thank you for giving me jobs.

30. Thank you for allowing me to live a life of my dreams.

Sleep Patterns

"If you can't sleep, then get up and do something instead of lying there worrying. It's the worry that gets you, not the lack of sleep."

Dale Carnegie

28th December, 2010

I woke up in the night around 12:45. I was wide awake. I decided not to fight the insomnia, as that never works. I thought I would do a bit of reading and spotted The Demartini Prophecy Manual, as I began recapping where I last left off, I began to read about the normal sleep. 6:00 Am. I smile to myself and thank John for relaying this. Instead of feeling that I am in some kind of abnormal and disturbing sleep pattern, I am actually in a normal pattern, designed to allow the body to adjust and carry out certain normal functions. Yeah!

No Income and feeling challenged!

"The ultimate measure of a man is not where he stands in moments of comfort, but where he stands at times of challenge and controversy."

Martin Luther King, Jr.

30th December, 2010

I'm feeling a bit wretched today, as well as tearful. I think it is fear of the future, and to a degree an overwhelming feeling. I am not going to be hard on myself though. After all, I have not worked for six weeks, I have no other income and I've spent hours applying for jobs in a system that gives no regard to the applicant. Yes, I am feeling sorry for myself and this is a definite no, no. I need to be more proactive. Okay, I will allow myself a bit of a cry; that way the body can relax. Others are worse off than me, and look how lucky I am to have the time to think and plan my book. I sure do appreciate money and what it can buy. I know how much more careful I am going to be when I start earning some again. I listened to Demartini's Financial Wealth guidance and perhaps now I will follow the lady who saved 17% of her earnings and never earned more than $2.50 per hour but ended up a multimillionaire from her investments.

It's funny, I picked up a book from the library and it was more out of curiosity but it's a book about Archangel Michael. I've seen his pictures and some cards in the mind, body, spirit shop in town so I was curious to find out more. As is normal for me I never start reading a book from the front cover, I always look to the back. If there is anyone who can explain that rationale to me I would love to hear from you! Anyway, as I read it the book intrigues me because she is saying that Archangel Michael is great if you are in a job you don't like and want to make a career change and are worried about money. So I stopped blubbing and decided to meditate on this fantastic guardian angel.

I quickly got my backside kicked and here I am motivated to continue writing the book. Funny coincidence though.

Happy New Year

"Cheers to New Year and another chance for us to get it right."
Oprah Winfrey

1ˢᵗ January 2011

As a new year begins I am full of love and optimism for the future.

Heartfelt Love

"It is very important to generate a good attitude,
a good heart, as much as possible. From this, happiness
in both the short term and the long term for both
yourself and others will come."
Dalai Lama

2ⁿᵈ January, 2011

It's amazing who you forget to send a greeting to, who sends you one, and who doesn't. At first I had a few disappointments, of my own making of course! That is, I had expectations that were not met by friends who were clearly taking their time up with higher valued activities. So what does that mean when I get someone valuing me and sending me a Happy New Year wish? It means that amazing things are happening and I am grateful for these wishes. It means that I was spending my time on high valued activities and that involved my family, my church, preparing invites as a thank you to people and relaxing at the boat club, listening to the sounds of the band. So no room for disappointment, everything is balanced.

At church I felt warmed by the sermon which was all about shining your light on people. I hope and pray that 2011 sees me shining my light on people and honouring the grand orderly design of the Universe. There was a baptism, and it was beautiful. It has taken billions of years for light from a star to seed and then create a baby, how precious and beautiful every baby and every human being is. I left church and met a friend for a catch up. On the way there, I saw one of my "cloud" patterns, it was a Koala bear, a lucky sign that all is well. I wanted to capture the photo however, we got stuck at the lights and by the time we could see it again, the clouds had moved and it didn't look like a Koala anymore.

To finish off the day I got a rare call from a cousin in England; that was special and ended the day with another heart warmed feeling. I am lucky, and I am thankful.

Post Traumatic Stress Disorder (PTSD)

"Our greatest glory is not in never falling,
but in rising every time we fall."

Confucius

8th January, 2011

A mixed day really. I was preparing for a BBQ tomorrow. Of the people I invited I am faced with letting go of a few friends and this I always find hard. I have to accept that I am now vibrating at a higher frequency and as such I will attract different people into my life. It's not that I no longer love my old friends or that they no longer love me, our values have changed and as such we seek to fulfil different voids. I must remember that respect, duty, helping a friend in need etc. are values instilled in me and which younger generations do not seem to hold as dear. I cannot change that and have no control over that. I feel sad, a need to let go, so on the flip side I am so grateful for receiving more lessons in letting go.

Today I was invited to the home page of PTSD. Well that struck a chord, personally because my serial losses are like a PTSD but again, it was synchronous with a friend who shared with me that her father went through PTSD.

Inspiration

"The fastest way to inspire someone is to be inspired."

Emily Gowor

10th January, 2011

This morning was lovely and inspiring. I read Emily Gowor's story of how her life has changed since she attended The Demartini Breakthrough. It's kind of how it is for me. Emily is only 23 years old and has already accomplished her early dreams. That is remarkable and should be enough of an indication as to how powerful this Demartini work is.

Inland Tsunami In Toowoomba

"'Inland Tsunami' hits Australian town; 10 dead, 72 missing. "Today it is tolerable, tomorrow is going to be bad and Thursday is going to be devastating,"

Campbell Newman

11th January, 2011

Last night there was an inland tsunami in Toowoomba and this morning we hear the news that eight have lost their lives and 70 or more are missing. My prayers are for all the families involved and without their homes. I so want to offer my assistance, crikey I am not working so I could help. Then I realise that it's not that easy, because I have my daughter to look after and I can't leave her.

Despair has set in, and I feel "without hope," anxious and totally rotten. A voice inside me says, how can you feel like that when there are families who lost their loved ones last night? So this thought bounces around my head and I look up "despair" on the Internet to find inspiration. I realise that the despair is to balance out the hope of the past seven weeks. I have remained hopeful and "positive" as I want to give the Universe the right message about work, but I guess it's reasonable to assume that after seven weeks of unemployment and faced with the Brisbane agency market I might feel a tad despairing.

Sunshine Again

15th January, 2011

Today the sunshine came back into my life. I did a load of spring cleaning and felt renewed. How lucky! I am thankful and grateful for my life, my home and everything I do. I called friends affected by the floods to see if I could offer help. I spoke to Emily and was inspired. I offered my friend Brenda the opportunity to work on her issues.

Frustration High

18th January, 2011

Today I am just waiting to hear back, waiting to hear back. We are going away for a week tomorrow so that should be enough to put any anxious thoughts out of my head. The weather was so hot and humid today which did not help. Mum suffered heat stroke on the golf course, that's how hot it was! I've told her that I don't want her to become one who's last day ended on the golf course. Though actually that must be a great way to go! Doing something you love.

Checking e-mails, checking for new jobs, chasing up agencies who have not yet returned my calls. I am so, so sick of it. Then I think, oops, I need to balance the thoughts out, I love being challenged and having the opportunity to prove my experience and skills. All applications and interviews give the opportunity to do this. Perseverance is the key. Do not give up and then the Universe will yield and offer you a great job.

Happy Holidays

21st January, 2011

The family have met up with our New Zealand friends on the Gold Coast. It's the upside of all that hard slog of looking for work. We had a lovely time catching up with Di and Debs and the family of dancers who were performing at Jupiter's on the Gold Coast. I have still not heard anything from the interview; does it mean good news or bad news?

Well, let me choose—it means good news, the Universe is clearly gambling to find me the best job it can and let's face it, in Australia most decision making is off put until another day despite what they say they are going to do.

In the past weeks with all the floods I am catching a glimpse of what makes the Australians the way they are, after all at any unexpected time, their worlds are turned upside down with life threatening situations and loss unimaginable. Mmm, I think I am learning a little about Aussie grit, it's quite admirable.

Gratitude for Life

28th January, 2011

Last night I was restless and dreaming vividly. My whole family lived in a large multi-storey house and there was a creek nearby. We were preparing for the river to rise but felt safe to a degree; I mean how far can the river truly rise? When it came it was crazy, like all the scenes witnessed on television during the floods is more than that even! We ran up the stairs and tried to find safety, I was scared, there seemed no end to the rising torrent of water and soon Mum & Dad and furniture were sweeping away. I cannot describe the terror, I was thinking this is it, this is it. I woke up and realised that my dream stemmed from the recent floods. I remembered that life is very fragile and that at any moment God can take our life just like that. I felt grateful to be alive and so, so lucky.

Horoscope hits the mark

29th January, 2011

Hi Lynn! Here is your **Daily Chinese Horoscope** for Saturday, January 29

Feelings of uncertainty and dissatisfaction with your career may weigh on you at this time. Try not to let depression tighten its grip on you. This can be hard, so be sure to carve out some time for leisure. Some free time and physical activity may be all you need to get through this slump.

Yesterday   Tomorrow

Did yesterday's scope hit the mark?   What does the future hold?

Double Cyclone

31ˢᵗ January, 2011

After feeling many tears and crying I felt as though I was creating the cyclone. This morning I had a session with mentor Rowan Burn. I was so grateful for the balance brought back into my life as the Category 5 Cyclone hit Northern Queensland.

DM Group HeartMath

5ᵗʰ February, 2011

I spent the day with other facilitators today. We often meet up to work through things together. Today, several facilitators were helping me to work The Demartini Method® on a stressful situation. Marcia Becherel, who is trained in HeartMath, was testing her equipment and so I was attached to an electrode which was measuring my stress levels. As we progressed through The Demartini Method®, it was amazing to see how the stress responses changed as I broke through the perceptions I had, proving electronically that The Demartini Method® works.

Demartini Event In Brisbane

22ⁿᵈ March, 2011

I was crewing tonight for Global 1. A most interesting evening because I am due to facilitate at the Brisbane Breakthrough Event at the weekend however, an issue has cropped up and it looks unlikely that I will be able to continue. I was feeling "charged" or rather cross and so yes, this is a sign that there are issues in play that need to be addressed. Boy, did it knock me however, inside there is a little voice saying that it's all okay Lynn, it's a good sign. When am I ever going to learn to listen to intuition? Am I that addicted to my ego?

Learning To Let Go

23ʳᵈ March, 2011

Gosh, I don't want to give up on facilitating. Global 1 tried talking to me and I was cross; I have put so much effort into doing my preparation and now facilitation is slipping away. Why don't they understand me? Why are they stopping me? Finally they have asked their head facilitator to speak to me. She has asked me a series of questions and has made the decision that I will not be facilitating at the next Breakthrough Event. She has given me an exercise to undertake and invited me to attend the Breakthrough Event instead. Reluctantly, I have to accept that I will not be facilitating. I feel really upset and puzzled, but I know that if I work the exercise, I will understand.

Chiropractic Support

24th March, 2011

Brian is great; he really inspires me to forge ahead with my mission. OPS is what he whispers to me about the brain noise in my head. He means "other people's shit" Clear instruction is to brush it aside. He worked some emotional freedom tapping on me and I have come away feeling lighter and more inspired. I am working through the exercise that Pam gave me to do and already I am seeing that it really doesn't matter whether I facilitate or not because there are equal benefits and drawbacks. If I keep working the method I will eventually reach the "aha" moment and pass through indifference.

Night Out

26th March, 2011

Friday was supposed to be a night in which I was embarking on Demartini facilitation only, if you recall, I was asked to attend instead. Part of my anger was the fact that I had booked a Hotel and did not really need it any longer. Anyway, I had completed the collapse and reached an "aha" moment, so I now realised that for a few hundred dollars, potentially I might be trading for something of equal, if not more, value to me.

Well, boy oh boy! I had a fantastic night out with two friends. It's something I don't get much chance to do and I really valued it. I felt contented and when I turned up for The Breakthrough Experience® I was able to chat and greet everyone who had been a party to changing the course of events and thank them. It was a genuine "thank you" and the benefit

I gained from The Breakthrough Experience® was again an almost magical one in which I could truly see how past events, and people from my past and present were "loving" me and helping me move forward in my transformation.

I cannot describe the power and beauty of these experiences. I want you to share them too, when you are ready of course. I owe so much to Pam Maxwell for being so present and strong and teaching me a little bit more about myself. Now I can see that there was nothing wrong in what happened. I can see that the Universe was taking me on a journey, and actually giving me a night off, so to speak. I feel well loved and warm and fuzzy.

And The Dominoes Came Tumbling Down

26th March, 2011

Today I was continuing to work the breakthrough on my sisters and so quickly and rapidly a whole piece of the puzzle unravelled, I was still having a "breakthrough. "The magic is continuing and I am in awe of this wonderful Universe and how it works. I am so grateful to Dr. J. F. Demartini. Move over Einstein!

Athol Macdonald

9th April, 2011

I attended a one day event in Brisbane, run by Rowan Burn. I had volunteered to assist and besides which, it was Rowan presenting and he is always inspiring to listen to. At the end he gave an opportunity to speak to the attendees and I really appreciated the offer to assist. Afterwards I talked to an ex Olympic rower called Athol Macdonald. It was inspiring to hear his personal story and his words seemed to come from the Universal spirit. I explained to him that I had been lacking in energy and he shared his story with me of how he could tap into an abundance of energy, the energy that helped him to win his rowing races and get him into the Olympic squad in 1976.

Church Sisters

21ˢᵗ April, 2011

It is Easter and I went to church for the full blown story over several days, of Christ dying and then rising. We had a symbolic last supper and I noticed that Lauren and I sat with two sisters of similar age to the twins. I felt so blessed by their company.

Light At The End Of A "Bad" Day

4ᵗʰ May, 2011

Today started on the wrong foot. I had a rush of anger, feeling undermined at work. That old repetitive pattern rears its ugly head. Of course! Is this the push to remind me of my true mission, just as it was in my last job and the one before? Have I not worked on this with method? I know this job is a tide-me-over until I can fly my business as a Demartini facilitator; however I have worked the method to find all the benefits of how this role is supporting my highest value and mission in life. So, do I really need to be experiencing this again? Clearly I do but the beauty came at the end of the day when I was figuratively told I was a "life saver." What lovely words and how I appreciated them.

23ʳᵈ May, 2011

I was freed from my job today for asking for my worth. I was aware of contract roles that I could do for more money and had expressed an interest in them. For some reason, I was not allowed to apply for them, nor earn more money. Again, the Universe was playing the dance card, time for me to move on to the next thing, so I thanked my boss. I surrender to the Universe and God this time.

> Hi Lynn! Here is your **Daily Chinese Horoscope** for Monday, May 23
>
> Consider this day to be lucky and special for you. Don't be afraid to venture into new investment and projects, because you'll likely succeed. Make the most out of this opportunity be doing a lot of activities.

Reporting In To the Chiropractor

24th May, 2011

Wow, I wrote quite a bit on my book. I was determined to turn the emotions of being let go into good. I was thankful to my boss; I know instinctively that he is acting for my good.

I went for my chiropractic session which was amazing. Brian said I was more relaxed than I had ever been. I credit that to the surrender process I was going through. Instead of fighting the fact that I had been treated unfairly, I accepted it. I was certain that my way forward was now going to be different and authentic. Lynn Hope Thomas is authentic. I want to feel like me, I want to feel true to me, I want to feel true to others. It's no wonder the Universe got me out of there!

Meeting Up

25th May, 2011

A friend suggested I look at meet-up and find a group that would give me the opportunity to speak. So I did and I booked. It was a lovely evening tonight. It started with some light, warm banter with a few lovely ladies, and then as the guest speakers came on, I had little expectation of what was going to happen. The first speaker was entertaining but nothing was really resonating, then in her final act, bang, her message was you have to be "You." Precisely where I am at and where I want to be! As the raffle was about to be drawn I said to the girl next to me, "It is going to be my number," and it was!

The second speaker was without doubt annoying me with his pommy jokes about rules! Interesting I thought, I must have a few charges there. Then bang, he hit me with, "You all have a song to be sung," and yes I do, it resonated. I forgave him for the pommy jokes.

Anyway, the evening reached a crescendo. I got to speak to writer who had written a book about fraud. This marvellous lady was sharing her story about how she ended up in prison for fraud, after trusting a partner. I explained to her some of my story and we talked for a while about The Demartini Method®. I told her about my twin sisters and my loss and how Demartini had woken me up to the fact that nothing is ever missing and how I was learning to recognise their traits around me etc. I also told her how, at my church's 'last supper' two little girls had joined our table and to me it was perfect, my sisters were there. She asked how old I was when they had died and was looking intrigued, perhaps a bit shocked. Never did I expect what happened next…she opened her book and said, "Can I show you my family? Here are my children and here are my twin daughters, they are now aged nine." It blew me away. The synchronicity blew me away. How grateful I am to God, the Universe and to Demartini for my wake up. Thank you heaven, it is all around if only we tune in to it.

Department of Public Works

July, 2011

The universe is constantly supporting and challenging me. Each are of loving service. My desire to earn more money was put into action by the challenge of losing an employment position to gaining a contract with an amazing bunch of people. This Team of dedicated people enjoy being at work, they make work a joy. I am grateful for the ambience and work ethic they adopt. Pity it's only a 6 week stint. I notice how I love the supporting environment, today they suggested I stay and take a fulltime position, but I know that support without challenge is not where my growth will come from.

Brisbane Stress Busters and A Rockstar

September, 2011

Working fulltime as a single mum certainly prepares me for many of life's challenges and teaches me to multitask. In my spare time I have grouped with several other facilitators to provide support to the flood affected people of Ipswich. In the lead up to the event I put my mind to thinking of ways to publicise the event. I also was aware that the Xfactor winner Altiyan Childs was doing a concert in Ipswich, but never did I imagine what came next. As we were running the group session, I heard his band practising across the street. In my excitement I ran out like a crazy fan and asked him to come and say a few words for the flood affected of Ipswich, which is graciously did. This man truly has a heart of gold. He came and spoke to the participants and allowed us to take photographs and a video. Everyone there enjoyed it. I felt amazed that I had powerfully manifested a rock star into my life.

CSC

October, 2011

Support and then challenge. Remember that. Remember that it is all for a reason and appreciate that whatever appears to be the challenge is actually a true gift. I smiled as I left CSC; I knew that all was not as it appeared. The Universe was saying right it's time to continue the book. I knew the role was crazy, I was working across two physical locations with two networks to log into and keep track of. I was not appreciating it and I could see that it was a reflection of me trying to work in my normal job role and also trying to begin a new career using the Demartini Method. It's crazy but I am determined I will do it.

New Job at Transpacific Industries

October, 2011

Today I knew when the phone rang it was the day I would be back in work. It was actually the 18th October 2011, the birthdate of the twins so I knew it! I've been working on the book for a few months and I must say it has been difficult not earning any income at all. I guess that is the power of the balance, the wealth is invested in this book. Yes! I can now build finance to support the next stages of the book and also pay for the cost of facilitating at breakthroughs.

Moving House

December, 2011

Okay it's time to move into temporary accommodation in Indooroopilly. This is hard work and disruptive to not only working, but to running a business. I feel so stretched but I know that better days will come.

Argh1 I feel like I have lost everything because I now have no network have all that name changing stuff to do. Benefits are that I get to remember all the things I need to do. Knowing I need to move house again in January 2012 is unthinkable right now. Anyone who has ever moved house will know where I am right now. I feel like I am falling backwards, however I know I am moving forwards.

The Love Boat

January, 2012

Here is the counter balance to the hard work involved in working long hours and moving house and losing momentum. I am here in Sydney about to embark on a Holland America cruise liner bound for the Fijian Islands. It's hard to disguise my excitement. I was totally appreciative; all my loved ones were with me, and little was I to realise how special a journey I would be taking. The ship was carrying another 500 passengers all who were attending Dr Wayne Dyer or a Hay House "Movers and Shakers" course.

Two weeks of being totally spoilt. All I can say is that meeting Dr. Wayne Dyer and having the pleasure to be in his company and with many other passengers of similar ilk was totally awesome. Dr Wayne Dyer was totally inspiring. Even the crew on the ship recognised that there was a lot of love on board. I met some amazing people with awesome stories who were attending the Hay House course being run by Reid Tracey and Cheryl Richardson.

Another special experience was in Vanuatu at the Cascade waterfalls, I felt totally at one with the environment, as I walked back to the taxi, I realised my body, mind and spirit were all at one, I had an inner glow that was radiating

Moving house again!

February, 2012

I am letting God carry me through this next move, I feel so stretched. It's hard to believe how many job and house moves I have gone through in the past 24 months. It feels like I am passing through a black hole. I remind myself that God is plotting out my path and it will all settle down. The benefits to me are I am paying off my debts from the last book writing exercise, I will soon be nearer to Town, and closer to many amenities and I am saving up to complete my book.

Perth Breakthrough Experience

February, 2012

Wow, despite working long hours at Transpacific, on average 50 hours a week, I am totally prepared to travel to Perth for a breakthrough weekend and catch a night flight so that I can be back at work on the Monday morning! Crazy. I will do whatever I need, to pursue my mission.

I am definitely being tested of my commitment to mission, working in this organisation is challenging, however with the benefit of the Demartini Method I can sail through it.

Brisbane Breakthrough Experience

March, 2012

Its breakthrough time again, I love being a facilitator and guiding people. I love meeting up with fellow Facilitators. We are extensions of Dr J F Demartini, the flow of energy is amazing.

Sydney Breakthrough Experience

April, 2012

Sydney Breakthrough has been amazing. John took a client through the grief process towards the end and I was mesmerised at how much can hold onto grief. The lady's shoulders were shaking as she cried and wailed in grief, but as John was lifting it, her shoulders would raise up, trying to hold it in her body, until eventually she had to let go, and in letting go smiles began to radiate across her face. The lines of grief replaced with peace. She left the stage at peace and smiling, admitting to the audience that the grief had gone. You'll find her testimonial at the front of the book. Her name is Adriana Virgo.

The Demartini Institute—Training Program

June, 2012

This is my third trainers in two years and this time round my experiences signify that my book is now ready for completion. A remarkable thing happened, my sister Janet spoke to me through another fellow trainer and it felt so right. It felt awesome. The lady was called Geraldine Moran and had written a book called "Miracles or Coincidences". It was amazing we looked at each other and it was as if some kind of telepathy was happening, I said something like' What is happening ?…it's like we are communication without speaking!'. Geraldine nodded and as I looked at her eyes, I saw Janet and she said "You see, Lynn, miracles really do happen" and in that very moment her words were present, true and incredible. If you recall back on page 10 as a child I was praying for a miracle on chicken wishbones! When you work the Demartini Method the ability to see the true light is amazing. I knew then that my contract with Transpacific would not be renewed; it was time to complete my book and help others to see the divine perfection and bring peace to their lives.

ACKNOWLEDGEMENTS

I wish to give my thanks and gratitude to all those who have made this book possible:

God for all that is.

My sisters Janet & Hazel Hope Thomas

Parents Bill and Jean Hope Thomas

Lauren my daughter

My ex-husbands and in particular to Lauren's father.

Daniela Stalling

Emma Hall

Dr. J. F. Demartini, fellow facilitators, and the Demartini Institute.

Deborah Cooper

Rowan Burn

Greg Klopper and the Global 1 Crew

Emily Gowor, the Word Artist, Book Mentor

Michael Beast for Book Design and Branding

Mark Stephen Pooler

Sunil Tulsiani PIC and Cora Cristobal TWC

Kris Whitehead—Think To Succeed

ABOUT THE AUTHOR

Lynn Hope Thomas is an Author, Keynote Speaker and Leader in transformation, Lynn works with organisations and leaders to dissolve the challenges that block progress, achieving the outcome of re-energizing teams to focus on the strategic aims and goals of the organization. Lynn is an expert in the transformation of emotional challenges, as she brings individuals to greater fulfilment, awareness and breakthrough at a fraction of the time if left to their own devices.

Lynn's credibility is built on solid pillars of experience and wisdom. Beginning with a career in Accountancy, Lynn transitioned after ten years to embracing IT Systems development and Software implementation, attaining a Master's Degree in Business Administration Information Technology (University of Central Lancashire, UK). Lynn continued to develop her consistent track-record in the fields of business analysis and Program & Project Management methodologies. Driven by her personal challenges with experiencing loss (including the death of her twin sisters and several relationship and career adversities), Lynn studies with Dr. John Demartini, world leading human behavioural expert, speaker and best-selling author to seek the most effective path to transformation. And is professionally-trained in the Demartini Method®—the tool with 1000 uses for empowering life, Lynn offers Key Note speeches, presentations and facilitation in this scientific and reproducible method to assist others to experience a rapid transformation and achieve their goals.

Lynn consults and presents one-on-one and group sessions to bring cohesive certainty to the challenges faced in today's fast-paced environment.

Offering resolution to specific challenges, Lynn performs initial assessment of the business requirements to determine the best course of action to achieve results. Lynn can provide annual and quarterly packages that can be tailored for Managers, Program Teams, or groups of employees, leading to a which transformed workforce, who are energised, productive and inspired employees. Lynn's candid approach and authentic style ensures that organisations benefit from growth, improved sales and customer/supplier relations, a focused workforce and strong co-worker relationships, clarity of purpose and vision.

Lynn helps leaders, entrepreneurs and individuals to break through difficulties they face with any situation around loss. Loss comes in many forms from personal, job or a financial loss. Lynn is devoted to helping organisations and individuals see the benefits that loss creates, ensuring that recovery is swift, reducing financial cost for the organisation, and minimizing the chance of repetition.

www.lynnhopethomas.com